WHAT THEY DIDN'T TELL ME

WHAT THEY *didn't* TELL ME

HOW TO BE A RESILIENT LEADER AND BUILD TEAMS YOU CAN TRUST

JAWAD AHSAN

LIONCREST
PUBLISHING

WHAT THEY DIDN'T TELL ME

How to Be a Resilient Leader and Build Teams You Can Trust

ISBN   978-1-5445-0942-6 *Hardcover*

978-1-5445-0940-2 *Paperback*

978-1-5445-0941-9 *Ebook*

978-1-5445-0943-3 *Audiobook*

To Ezz and Dia

Lead and love—the choice is always yours.

CONTENTS

INTRODUCTION

"DUDE, THEY'RE TALKING ABOUT YOU ON NPR!"

Text messages. Email. Voicemails. Slack.

I woke up to notifications across them all.

I was on Pacific Standard Time, but the market had already opened on the East Coast. The Securities and Exchange Commission (SEC) made public that morning the fact that they had been sending letters via email to Axon, addressed to me, with what had been fairly routine questions about our financials.

That is to say the questions were routine—at first. They included fairly innocuous themes, such as clarifying how we calculate our backlog, explaining our revenue recognition policy for our recently introduced subscription programs, or disclosing how we allocate goodwill across our reportable segments. Hardly headline-grabbing material.

Now, it should go without saying that when the SEC asks you questions, benign or not, you respond immediately. For a company to get actual letters from the SEC is rare. They had begun sending them to us in May of 2017, a month after I'd joined the company as chief financial officer (CFO).

It was now October.

My predecessor, who was registered with the SEC as CFO of Axon, had left abruptly. The SEC first attempted to reach out to the prior CFO with their questions, but he obviously wasn't there to receive them. When they didn't receive a response, they called into the company directly, asking to speak to him. It was then that the receptionist informed the SEC that the previous CFO was no longer with the company and that I had replaced him. The SEC then, of course, asked to speak with me.

This is where we encountered problem number one.

Our company fields a countless number of calls from

people wanting to speak to either me or Rick, our CEO, usually to sell us something. As such, we empower our front desk staff to act as aggressive filters so that we don't end up on the phone all day fielding pitches. However, we realize—now—that some clarity about *how* aggressive to be in said filtering might have been in order. When the SEC asked to speak to me, the receptionist said no. When they made it clear that they were the SEC and *had* to speak with me, she said, "I'm sorry, but you're not getting through to him. Here is his email."

To be fair, she was doing exactly as she had been told, and because she was our filter, I never knew these calls had come in. The representative from the SEC had no option but to use the email the receptionist had provided.

This is where we encountered problem number two.

I also have an equally aggressive spam filter for my inbox. I set it up in that way because when I began my transition into the new position, the company issued a press release. As a result, I was bombarded with emails from various outlets reading along the lines of, "Congratulations on the new position! We'd like to talk to you about X, Y, or Z" (again, trying to sell me something). The spam filter was set to look for the slightest discrepancies to ensure that I didn't receive any more of those kinds of messages.

The filter found one such discrepancy in the name of the SEC representative and her corresponding email address. So the filter did what it was theoretically supposed to do and sent the first email containing the SEC's initial letter to my spam folder. That was in August.

The next one came at the beginning of September.

Then another at the end of September.

That third email had a different letter attached than the previous two had—one decidedly less cordial. It warned me that if I didn't respond to the message, the SEC would have no choice but to take their questions—and my lack of response—public via their EDGAR system.

EDGAR is a website the SEC uses for the disclosures of all publicly traded companies. When a public company files their quarterly and annual reports or issues a press release, they have to give everyone the same information at the same time. This is to ensure no one has an advantage when it comes to trading the company's stock. The SEC uses EDGAR to help facilitate this. If someone follows Axon—be they investors, analysts, or reporters—they receive an alert from EDGAR when a piece of information regarding the company hits the site.

The SEC published all three letters.

A material weakness is a term that essentially means the controls in your finance organization are so weak that you may have to issue a restatement somewhere down the road. A restatement means a company reported numbers that were so wrong they have to be restated. This is one of the worst things that can happen to a publicly traded company because it tells investors they can't trust your published financials.

When I joined Axon, we had *three* material weaknesses. One of the main reasons I was brought on as CFO was to fix them. After I joined the company in April of 2017, our stock started to climb because of the increased discipline I was bringing to the organization. This increased the confidence of our investors; they believed that I was going to be able to set things right. People felt like we knew what we were doing. That said, the specter of these weaknesses was already looming over our company when the SEC published the letters.

Our stock tanked the minute the SEC published those letters to the EDGAR system. Some investors wanted to sell off Axon shares before something even worse than an SEC investigation occurred. All of that goodwill I had worked to build was evaporating before my eyes, as people were washing their hands of us.

AXON ENTERPRISE INC (NASDAQ: AXON)
MONTH OF OCTOBER 2017

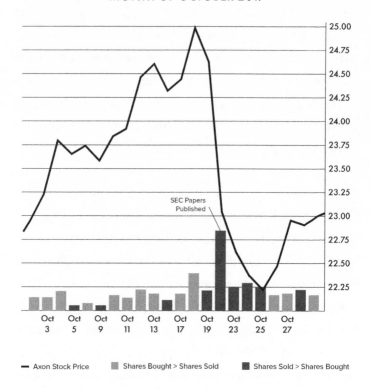

SEC Papers
Published

— Axon Stock Price   ▒ Shares Bought > Shares Sold   ■ Shares Sold > Shares Bought

Within a matter of days, the threats of shareholder law-suits came. There are law firms out there that specifically track these kinds of events—some call them "ambulance chasers." If a stock falls for a reason they can point to as negligence on the part of the company, they send out feel-ers to shareholders who might want to pursue a lawsuit. When they saw the reason for our stock drop was that we—that I—didn't respond to emails from the SEC, these law firms swooped right in. All told, more than *twenty* firms announced they were seeking investors who might want to start procedures to file suit.

I was usually awake by 5:00 a.m. PST because my children are up early, but as it happened that particular morning, I had a chance to sleep in. By the time I woke up that day in Arizona, the market was already open on the East Coast and our stock was taking a nosedive. When I saw the EDGAR release, I told myself there was no way I could have done what they said I had done. I opened my email, searched "SEC.gov," and there were the three emails in my spam folder.

Unopened.

Immediately, I reached out to the SEC. When I finally got a hold of someone there, I apologized profusely for missing the emails. I also asked her if they had considered sending the letters via some other method, including snail mail. She told me that the SEC *used* to be in the practice of sending both email *and* certified snail mail letters, but for some reason, "they just stopped." She did admit that since they'd stopped that practice, they had incidents like this one where the emails had gone unnoticed "from time to time."

I felt the floor fall out from underneath me. I thought that not only did this mean the end of my career at Axon, it meant the end of my career *period*.

It didn't take long for the media to pick up the story. Articles started hitting the web by midday. The next morning, I received a call from our executive vice president of product at the time.

"Dude, they're talking about you on NPR!" he said.

"What did they say?"

"Oh, just that you were ignoring the SEC."

Insert forehead slap. Needless to say, that was *not* how I envisioned making the news with this company.

It wouldn't have been out of the realm of reason for Axon to disavow me. Here I was, a brand-new CFO, and by all appearances, it looked like I had dropped the ball in a major way. Our CEO had every right to fire me, and my team had every right to abandon me.

But that's not what happened.

My team rallied around me. We'll talk more about how and why they did this in the coming pages, but what's important to note here is that they did. Despite everything that had occurred, they believed in me as a leader and went into crisis mode to support me and, in a broader sense, the company.

ARE YOU RESILIENT? IS YOUR TEAM?

A common thread I see in new leaders today is that they tend to focus only on what needs to be accomplished. They feel their role as a leader is to simply find direct reports who can fill a role and perform the duties of that job.

What they don't do is focus on the person themselves and why they're a good fit. Of course, you have to look for the specific skills associated with a position, but in order to build a team you can trust, those skills are table stakes. Your people also need to be a good cultural fit. How else can you rest assured that when the chips are down, your team will have the resiliency and willingness to follow you into the breach?

The truth is that there are some things you can coach and other things you can't. I've seen so many leaders waste time and effort on the uncoachables. Trying to coach a direct report into being a person they're not is a waste of time.

In my experience, there are four uncoachable traits:

- Unyielding integrity: Always doing what's right and holding others to the same standard.
- Accountability: Fostering trust, executing with a sense of urgency, and taking pride in the quality of your work.
- Collaboration: Being a team player and always priori-

tizing the well-being of the team above any individual achievement.

- Positivity (which goes beyond optimism): Being a positive thinker, breaking through barriers to present solutions, and not engaging in any gossip or negative talk; assuming positive intent and getting any issues or concerns out in the open.

While this might seem like common sense, far too often, I've seen leaders hire for skills, thinking they can train these traits into their direct reports. I've watched many leaders suffer for this belief.

When you hire people who inherently possess the uncoachable traits, you're free to coach them on the coachable skills and traits. When you become more of an advisor to your team than a manager—when you can trust and guide them instead of micromanaging them—you're well on your way to creating the team that will carry you and your company through the most challenging of times, and you can watch them accomplish great things.

But how do you do it?

HOW I DID IT

The things that I'm able to articulate as a leader come from a very unique set of specific experiences that I've had in my career thus far. I've learned not only how to build great teams but how to become an effective leader in the process.

Though I'm the CFO of a publicly traded company, my path there was anything but typical. I'm not a CPA. I never worked on Wall Street. Instead, I got a heavy dose of financial and leadership training from General Electric. This training lasted for more than thirteen years and occurred all over the world. I've traveled to thirty-six different countries and lived in seven. After General Electric, I went to work at a private-equity-backed company. While this was an incredible experience, it required a steep learning curve.

Which is to say I had my share of fuck-ups, but I learned from every one of them. I want to share those lessons with you.

Just as importantly, I look, feel, and talk like the new and increasingly diverse workforce demographic. I am Pakistani American, the son of two immigrants, and a practicing Muslim. As you'll soon see, my background had an impact on my journey from where I began to where I am today. I bring a unique perspective to team building, leadership, and cultural development. The undeniable truth is that while the business world is changing, that change is slow. We still work in a straight, white-male-dominated industry. As diversity increases, attitudes and paradigms must shift as well. This is not just about checking boxes, though; in fact, taking this tactic can be downright damaging.

As an effective leader, you must be acutely aware of these changes and shifts in the world around us and, thus, in the workforce. This is particularly true when it comes to building your team and leading the way toward the culture you want to establish for them. There is more than a good chance that the people sitting around your table are not going to look or talk like you, and it's crucial that they feel welcome in their seat, regardless.

As I share with you how I faced these challenges in my own path, I hope to teach you how to look around the corner so that you can spare others from facing similar challenges as they go through their own journey on your team.

If you're looking for a survey of state-of-the-art management and business best practices, put this book down now. Similarly, if you're looking for tools or specific strategies, this isn't the book for you.

This book is my story, which, while unique to me, is rich and high stakes enough to provide some universal lessons. If you're down to join me on this journey, you might find that my experiences are similar to yours.

Are you in?

Then let's go back to the year 2000, where my leadership journey began.

CHAPTER ONE

"ENJOY THE TRIP TO NEW YORK"

In the fall of 2000, I was a senior in college at Holy Cross. I was applying for jobs and getting ready to enter the workforce. In our career planning center, there were the typical computers hooked up to the internet, but then there was also a wall full of wooden boxes. It looked like an old mill system. On these boxes were the names of different companies, and you could drop your résumé in the box if you wanted to apply to them. This was way before the days of online job applications.

I had a stack of résumés printed out. I dropped them off in the boxes for Goldman Sachs, J.P. Morgan, and all of the other Wall Street companies that were around at the time. Once I'd blanketed the boxes with my CVs, I saw that I had one left. I didn't want to keep it, so I looked for an extra one to dump it in.

"General Electric," I said. "I know them. They sell appliances—or whatever." And I dropped it in.

The thing was, I had zero interest in General Electric (GE). I literally only knew them as an appliance company. It was good that I even knew *that* much about them.

Because I got rejected by every other place I applied.

All except GE and Accenture, a consulting company.

I decided to attend an information session GE was holding the night before the interviews. At that session, they talked about the entire breadth of the company. I was blown away. I didn't realize they had their hand in jet engines, power turbines, and healthcare. It was a *huge* company, of which appliances were only a very small part. They had a massive financial services division as well, almost as big as some of the investment banks I wanted to work at. I couldn't believe it.

Then they spoke about their leadership development program, specifically their Financial Management Program. They had a number of functional programs, including ones for information technology and human resources.

Finance was the oldest one, dating back to 1914. It's one of the oldest, if not the oldest, financial leadership development programs in the country. It's the one most companies pattern their own after. In fact, GE's other functional programs have their foundation in the finance program.

Needless to say, I was impressed by the pedigree. I was hooked. I wanted this job.

In the interview the next day, I was asked, "If you had the choice of applying in any one of GE's businesses, which would it be?" At the time, GE owned NBC. Keep in mind, this was 2000, going into 2001—right in the prime of the Must See TV era. *Friends* was in its heyday, and NBC's headquarters was located in 30 Rock—Rockefeller Center—where everyone wanted to work. When all the interviewees were talking amongst each other, it seemed like everyone was putting in to work at NBC.

Not me, however. I was never the type of person to get starstruck. I was focused on learning. I wanted to work at GE for a couple of years and then leave to get my MBA, so I told them I had no interest in working at NBC. The interviewers were surprised by this and asked me why.

"I feel like everyone wants to go there for the big lights," I told them, "but I honestly don't care about that. I want to go where I can learn the most."

There were forty people in the room at the information session the night before. They were only going to select ten to go to the different business units and interview.

They picked me to go to NBC.

I decided to trust that someone there made the right call, but it was hard to see that at the time. Still, I got myself ready for the interview. I had to fly out the night before. Now keep in mind, I was a college senior. I grew up middle class. This is to say that up until that moment, people weren't flying me *anywhere*. GE flew me from Boston to New York, where I'd take a car to the hotel in Manhattan where they were putting me up for a couple of nights. It was a big deal for me.

One of my close friends from high school was visiting with me at Holy Cross the week before I was to leave for this incredible trip. We were talking about the whole experience and what it could be like. At the end of the conversation, as we were preparing to say goodbye, I said to him, "What if, after all of this, I don't get the job?"

"Well, then" he said, "just enjoy the trip to New York."

We parted ways and I headed to New York.

LOOK AT THAT VIEW

There were twelve candidates including myself, all from different colleges. We were at 30 Rock for a full day of interviews at NBC headquarters on what felt like the very top floor. The office was full of cubicles, and each one had a television in it. They were all, of course, tuned to NBC.

"Welcome to NBC," they told us at the beginning of the interviews. "You all are here to interview for the Financial Management Program, or FMP. At the end of the day, we're only going to select two of you of you to meet with our CFO, Mark Begor."

Keep in mind, I had been on interviews before, but not at this level—certainly not for jobs that required I wear a suit. The suits I did own were from the time I worked at Sears in high school, and I wore them mostly to weddings. The only one I had that didn't need to be dry-cleaned was this hideous olive-green color. I'm a tall guy, and I looked like the Jolly Green Giant. To top it off, the person who used to cut my hair wasn't available before the trip, so I had to get it from someone else, and it was *awful*.

Did I mention that right before the trip, I got strep throat? Yeah, that happened too. My doctor told me I probably shouldn't fly, but that clearly wasn't an option. He gave me medication with the warning that it was quite strong and to only take it early in the day or late at night—not the middle of the day because it would make me drowsy. Before you judge me, keep in mind that this was two decades before coronavirus or social distancing—back then, you powered through it. I'd be doing that interview over Zoom if it were held today.

So I'm in New York with my terrible haircut, ugly suit, and throat infection, and they tell us we're in for a pretty intense day.

Believe it or not, even with that stacked deck, things went fairly well. At the end of the day, someone pulled me aside to tell me that I had done well and that they were going to send me on to meet with Mark—me and one other woman. They told us that he wasn't ready to meet yet, so they were going to give us a breather, as we had been in back-to-back interviews all day.

I waited in a large conference room when in walked Lynn Calpeter. Lynn was Mark's number two, his vice president of finance, and was a high-profile executive who went on to become the CFO for GE Power. I didn't know this at the time, but I should have. I thought she was just some woman from the company who was spending time with me before I met with Mark.

It was around this time that my medication was starting to wear off.

The conference room had a gigantic window overlooking Central Park. I had never been to Manhattan, and there I was, on the top floor of 30 Rock, looking out over the city. It was incredible, but I was really starting to feel the effects of my medication waning. I leaned on a table near the window.

"Are you okay?" Lynn asked.

"No, I came here sick, and my medication is starting to wear off," I told her.

"Do you need to take some more?"

"No, it's going to make me drowsy, and I'm about to meet the CFO."

Then she said something completely disarming. "Look at this view," she said. There was a friendliness to it that put me at ease. She pointed out some landmarks and got me to feel a little looser, a little better about myself.

Just at that moment, they told me Mark was ready to meet me.

The handlers walked us over to his office. They asked me to sit down in one of the chairs outside the door as the other candidate went in. They told us we'd have about five to ten minutes each. I sat across from Mark's administrative assistant and tried to make small talk. And I waited.

I waited for five minutes. Then ten minutes. All the while, my illness was making me feel worse and worse, and the admin could see it.

"Any minute now," she said with a smile.

After twenty minutes passed, she got up from her desk and popped her head into the CFO's office to ask if they were almost done.

I strained to hear his answer but couldn't.

The admin came back out and said, "Okay, he's almost done."

A half hour passed. Finally, the other candidate came out, followed by Mark. She was all smiles. So was he. They shook hands and she walked away. Mark turned to me, still smiling, and invited me into his office.

I was cooked. My throat had razor blades in it, and I was sweating. I was ready to go home.

The view in his office was even more incredible. While the other conference room overlooked Central Park, his was on the other side of the building looking into downtown, with the most perfect view of the World Trade Center, something I had only seen in photos before.

"That's an amazing view," I said to him.

"Please have a seat," he said. There was a tone in his voice that said, "Look, stay focused."

The interview lasted five minutes. I was in such a daze that I don't even recall what exactly he asked me. At one point, seemingly midquestion, he stood up and said, "Well, if we make you an offer, I hope you'll consider it."

I stood up as well and said, "Yeah, absolutely. I'd love to be here." Then I shook his hand and showed myself out.

This all took place just before Christmas break, so I headed back to Boston. My family flew to Pakistan for a couple of weeks to visit family there. Recall again that this was the year 2000. I couldn't just check my email on my phone about whether or not I'd gotten the position. My best bet was to find an internet café, but my father's family were all farmers, and they didn't live close to the city. Truth be told, I was expecting to hear back before I left for my trip. The fact that I didn't left me with no small amount of anxiety.

While I was waiting, doubt started to creep in—not about

how I interviewed but if I had even made the right decision for my career.

"ARE YOU GOING TO BE A TEACHER?"

If you're a first-generation American whose parents originally came from South Asia, chances are they strongly urged you to become either a doctor or an engineer—and not just your parents but the community at large. So, not thinking much of it, I went into my freshman year at Holy Cross as a premed major.

Almost immediately, I hit a brick wall. The first class I had to take was advanced chemistry, and I struggled—greatly. It was particularly embarrassing for me because my father has his master's in chemical engineering. I stuck with it as long as I could, but after getting a few Cs, I realized I had to cut my losses, or my GPA would never recover.

Toward the end of my freshman year, I had a conversation with a senior who lived in my hall who always gave me great advice. I shared with him that I was feeling lost and was not sure what to choose for a major. He said to go with whatever class I had the best grade in, as it probably meant I enjoyed it the most.

That's how I ended up as an economics major. I absolutely loved how you could look at a big picture and broad themes but also dive as deep as you wanted and understand how tinkering with the low-level details had an effect on the overall system. I tend to be very much a big-picture thinker but act with an obsession for getting the details right.

After my freshman year, at a gathering with some family friends also of Pakistani descent, we were talking about our various academic pursuits. Someone asked how my premed studies were going, and I quietly mentioned that I had switched to become an economics major. After some awkward glances, someone snickered.

"What are you going to do with that, become a teacher?"

I stayed quiet because the truth was that I didn't have any idea of what I was going to do with an economics major. While others had landed summer internships at hospitals or were taking advanced engineering courses, I was gearing up for a prestigious gig working in the men's department at Macy's. (For me, Macy's was a big step up from Sears.)

With all of this self-doubt swirling in my head, the silence from GE was increasingly hard to take. One afternoon toward the end of our trip, I was finally able to make my way to an internet café. I logged in and saw the email I had been waiting for.

One of the people from GE who interviewed me on campus was a Holy Cross alum who had graduated a year ahead of me. He was one of the ones who decided I had interviewed well enough to go on to a coveted interview at NBC.

"You didn't get the spot at NBC," he told me, "but you did so well that they want to make you an offer to join the program at GE Plastics in Pittsfield, Massachusetts."

Remember how I said the most important thing was that I ended up someplace I could learn? Yeah, well, I had gotten so hyped up by being at NBC and taking in the atmosphere that I told him, "I'm not going to work for some plastics company." I was supposed to go from 30 Rock to the Rust Belt? From television studios to chemical plants? "Sorry, dude," I said, "but I'm going to pass."

At that point, I had already had an offer from Fidelity Investments, where I had interned previously, so I told him I was going to accept that position. It wasn't a great job, but my ego was bruised.

Thankfully, he realized I was being an idiot and wrote me back.

"I know you're disappointed," he said, "but trust me, this is a blessing in disguise. NBC is a posh location, but you're going to learn so much more at Plastics."

It snapped me to. That was what I said I had wanted in the first place, and I was grateful to him for the reminder, so I accepted the position with the GE Plastics program.

ENJOY THE RIDE

Whether you're already a leader or on your way up the ladder, it's important to take stock of your perceived setbacks. I say "perceived" because they might, in fact, be that blessing in disguise that my fellow Holy Cross alum pointed out to me.

If you find yourself in a situation where things didn't work out as you hoped, you can't allow yourself to become embittered and act out of spite. There's a saying about cutting off your nose, and it's absolutely true. Don't allow what you see as a slight to fill you with a self-righteousness that might lead to your ultimate failure.

When I took the job at GE Plastics, I spent my first two years in the development program, and I learned an incredible amount—so much, in fact, that I never did the standard rotation at the division headquarters because I felt it would detract from what I was gaining out in the field. While most of my friends from college went to go live the dream in big cities, I spent my first two years out of college at chemical plants in places like Mount Vernon, Indiana. Those experiences let me go hands-on with people on the manufacturing floor. I was given big jobs because I was a big fish in a small pond, so to speak. Because I had chosen to stay in Plastics, my last rotation was working in the same plant where Jack Welch—the former CEO of GE in its heyday from 1982 to 2001—had gotten his start.

At that site, I reported to the head of FP&A—financial

planning and analysis—who reported to the CFO for the entire site. I wanted to meet with him to discuss how the rotation would be structured because I had high expectations for myself. I wanted to apply to the Corporate Audit Staff program, an accelerated leadership development program reserved for the cream of the crop of all of GE's different functions.

A week into the rotation, my manager told me he'd resigned. The CFO realized that this was going to be a huge job to backfill and it would take time to find the right candidate, so he tapped me to step in and do the work in the meantime.

I became the interim head of FP&A for a billion-dollar business at age twenty-three, reporting directly to the CFO.

The chances of something like that happening at NBC were none—forget about slim. If I had wallowed in my feelings of being slighted, I would have missed out on an opportunity that definitively changed the trajectory of my career. Thankfully, that friend from Holy Cross reminded me what I was in this for, and it brought to mind the advice my high school buddy had given me before the trip—the same advice I'll share with you: enjoy the ride.

No, I didn't get the job at NBC, but I finally got to see New York City, flown in by a gigantic company and put up in a beautiful hotel. I got to see Times Square and Central Park, and spent time at 30 Rockefeller Plaza.

More importantly, I got to see the blessing in disguise that the Plastics opportunity was. The things I learned in that experience were invaluable.

Reflecting on that moment has served me well in my leadership journey. It's given me a short-term memory when it comes to negativity. I have a tendency to block it out—not when it comes to those things that demand my attention but during the times when I tried my hardest and things didn't quite work out. I have a filter now that allows me to see the silver lining in those situations. It's made me open and able to be objective about my failures, which turns them into learning experiences.

So many of us, especially those with leadership aspirations, want to focus only on the things that go right and tend to ignore the things that went wrong. If you want to succeed as a leader and become one that your teams will follow, you must embrace your failures. Take the time to unpack what happened—in an unemotional way—and figure out why something didn't work out. Think about what you could have done differently. If you predispose yourself to look at these things in a negative light, then you'll resist reflecting on them, and you'll lose the lesson within them.

YOU HAVE A CHOICE

In the same ways you have the ability to choose how you frame your successes and your failures, you also have the choice to step up and actually be a leader, not just say you want to be one.

This was a distinction I had to learn on my journey. In the next chapter, I'll tell you how someone helped me to do just that.

CHAPTER TWO

"BE A LEADER THIS WEEK"

In 2003, after my time in the plastics division, I was selected to go to another leadership program called the Corporate Audit Staff.

It started off with a weeklong boot camp and is considered a step up from the functional programs in GE. They were looking for the top performers from each of those programs for the Corporate Audit Staff, which was made up of anywhere from four to five hundred people.

The organization was structured as a classic pyramid. You came in as an associate and signed up for a two-year commitment. There was a promotion from year one to year two. Instead of doing four six-month rotations during your first two years, you did three rotations for every year you were in the program—and not just in one business. It was throughout all of GE's businesses.

That meant you could be sent to do a financial audit, a process audit, an operational audit—whatever they felt was needed. In actuality, it was more like GE's internal consulting arm than a classic audit function, which is why it was seen as such a career accelerator—you essentially were in an internal consultant role.

The vast majority of those four to five hundred people were associates. The company would take roughly 10 percent of them and promote them to audit managers. Of those audit managers, approximately 10 percent would be selected to become senior audit managers. Then, from that pool, around 30 percent were promoted to executive audit managers. Once at that level, you were an executive in the company.

Allow me to put that in perspective.

By the time you reach the executive auditor position, you're about seven years into your career at GE. Again, you're an executive in one of the largest companies in the world. Some people can come in and work twenty-five years and never be an executive.

This is to say that everyone in these leadership programs

was trying to get to top of that structure because it put your career on the fast track. As such, the first week of Corporate Audit training was full of type A personalities. They all knew what was at stake, and they were all very good at what they did because they had to be just to get in the room.

To describe the environment as hypercompetitive would be an understatement. I was fortunate enough to have a mentor there, Matt Cribbins. He was another graduate from Holy Cross, about six years ahead of me. He had already reached the level of executive audit manager. We sought each other out at my orientation because we knew each other, not just from college but from crossing paths during recruiting.

The very beginning of our training week, he stopped in to say hello to everyone. After he had done so, he pulled me aside.

"Be a leader this week," he told me.

I didn't know what he meant or what to say, so I just looked at him.

He said it again. "Be a leader this week."

At the time, I already thought of myself as a leader, so I

didn't think much of it—particularly because everyone else in that room already thought of themselves in the same way.

I later understood that what he meant was that I had a choice. I had to choose to be a leader. You don't just assume that because you're in a leadership position that you *are* a leader. It was the first time someone presented the idea in a way where it felt like it was a choice.

It didn't matter which role I was in. Anyone could have a title. I could have been named the CEO of GE the next day, and everyone would listen to me simply because of the three letters behind my name. You give someone an impressive-sounding role and power, then everyone has to do as they say.

But there's a huge difference between *having* to listen to someone and *wanting* to listen to someone. Having a title doesn't automatically make that happen. In fact, I'd argue that leading with the mentality that people have to listen to you will make them want to do the opposite.

If you want to build a team that is resilient and has a strong desire to follow you into the breach, you have to change your mindset about your position. A title is what you get when you earn your way into a job. You have to choose what *kind* of leader you're going to be once you've assumed that position.

How will you inspire people? How will you motivate them? These things must be a conscious choice.

With that realization, I had to ask myself: *What would I do differently?* He didn't give me any advice as to *how* to be a leader that week, just to *be* one. I was surrounded by people who were all looking to stand out that week—to be noticed. While I can't be sure, I believe my mentor wanted to be sure that I didn't blend in with the background— something that would have been easy to do in a group of high performers.

From that day forward, I volunteered for the hard things. Whenever we were placed on teams and given assignments, I'd raise my hand and ask for the toughest ones. It became a behavior that flavored my entire career. When there is something that no one else wants to do, I'm the guy that takes it on. It quickly became a strength for me—taking sticky, hairy problems or ambiguous goals and executing against them, bringing clarity to them, and moving the needle.

I've been told on more than one occasion that I'm cocky, and I believe it started in that week. The truth is I wasn't, and I'm not. I never grew up with any kind of confidence. That orientation was the first time in my life where I believed I had a choice I could make. I could choose to be confident, to speak up and ask questions, to make comments, and to share insights. I believed I could make my voice heard.

It didn't end in orientation week. When you're on these audits, you're still working with some of the same people, just in smaller groups. Everyone was still trying to one-up each other. It pushed me to continue to ask questions and share my opinions or take on that difficult task. It helped me to realize that I didn't have to let my life or career simply happen to me—I could choose the direction of both.

With my newfound confidence, in that first year, I had an opportunity to take a year-end audit in healthcare. It was one of the most challenging audits you could sign up for, and I wanted it specifically because it was hard. Once you get to senior audit manager and above, you stop rotating through all the different businesses, and I didn't want to miss this opportunity.

Matt Marsh was the senior audit manager in healthcare, and I wanted to work on his team. He had a reputation for being a tough guy to work for, which only made me want to run toward that business even more.

It was there that I'd learn one of the most powerful leadership lessons of all.

CHAPTER THREE

"I WILL DO EVERYTHING IN MY POWER TO MAKE SURE YOU'RE FIRED"

The audits were structured a bit differently than our business rotations in the leadership programs. Instead of the four-month arrangement, you'd do two three-and-a-half-month audits and then a five-month audit at the end of the year, specifically because the year-end audit tended to be a big one. It typically began in September and ran through the end of the year. It was structured as such so that we'd see two quarter closes and then the end of the year.

Healthcare was a huge business for GE then, and as of the

writing of this book, still is. Forty auditors would descend on Milwaukee for a five-month stint. As auditors, we lived in that city for five months, put up by the company in corporate apartments. The auditors ranged from their mid- to late twenties. We were young, in a fun environment, working with talented people, and essentially living together for almost half a year.

Once in Milwaukee, there was a kickoff dinner held for us. Matt Marsh was at this dinner, and everyone there was more or less in awe of him. He had a terrific persona and his piercing blue eyes and platinum hair lent him a ton of commanding, executive presence. He was incredibly smart and had a sterling reputation in the company.

All told, there were about forty people in the room for this dinner. It was a nice restaurant, and everyone had already had a few drinks. Everyone was excited about the upcoming five months. Matt spoke about his expectations and his ground rules for the next few months.

"You all are descending on this community," he said. "You're living in that apartment complex, but there are other people living there too. I want you to be respectful of these people. You're going to be out and about, enjoying the town of Brookfield, but you don't live here.

"Similarly, when you're in the office, you're going to be

building relationships with the people who work there. Some of you are going to cycle through here for a few months and then move on to something else. I'm staying here. I've got to maintain relationships. So I want you to be good representatives of not only the audit staff but of my team. I don't want to hear about any lapses in judgment on travel expenses, because we're all on the company expense policy with a corporate credit card.

"Above all, I expect every single one of you to have and exhibit an unyielding sense of integrity. If any one of you crosses that line or does anything to violate my trust, or the trust that the company has placed in you, I will do everything in my power to make sure that you are fired."

He let that statement hang in the air.

Keep in mind, we're in this nice restaurant, all having a good time, and all forty of us fell dead silent. He looked around to each and every one of us. None of us had a thing to say.

He set the tone. His doing so was one of the reasons the healthcare teams were so high-performing. We'd hear other stories from other locations about auditors going to bars and getting drunk. In fact, there was an infamous one about an auditor who was severely inebriated and harassing a woman, and when she refused his advances, he asked her, "Don't you know who I am? I work for GE! I'm a big-time auditor."

Needless to say, she called GE the next day. The guy had actually given her his card, which she used, and promptly got him fired.

INTEGRITY IS UNCOACHABLE

None of that happened in Milwaukee. People were too afraid to step out of line. For me, Matt taking that hard line really drove home the importance of integrity. It wasn't that I didn't already understand that it was necessary, but I hadn't yet articulated the idea that there were certain qualities in people that were uncoachable, that some people have an innate sense of integrity or they don't.

This doesn't mean that those without are always sloppy drunks who hit on local women in bars. However, those people who cut corners and look to take shortcuts in their work that undermine the quality of what they and their team are doing are demonstrating sure signs of a lack of integrity.

A prime example of this uncoachable quality occurred in that very same audit just a few months after Matt had made his declaration.

Halfway through the audit, we had what we called pilots—

people who come on for a one-month stint to essentially try out. They're given a short-term assignment. If they do well, then they're made an offer. It's not a position one can simply apply for and get in. The candidate has to be nominated. Once they get that nomination, they'll participate in the pilot and be assessed as to how they perform in that environment. As simple as that all sounds, it's quite a rigorous process.

One woman came into the program from a GE business in France, and she struggled right out of the gate. It was easy to tell within the first week whether or not someone was going to make it, and things weren't looking good. Then, all of a sudden, in her third week, she started uncovering issues in the business, all over the place, to the extent that it got people talking. People would say, "Did you hear what she found today? She found several big financial adjustments that needed to be booked."

As an auditor, you ultimately want to help the business, but you also are incentivized to make a name for yourself. If you find something that doesn't sit well, you have the business book an adjustment. Everyone is trying to win that rat race. Finding issues in an audit was an almost surefire way to get promoted. If you sailed through one and didn't find anything, there was an unspoken implication that maybe you just weren't that good at your job because there's *always* something to find. There were literal cash awards given to auditors who found glaring issues, and it created a somewhat cutthroat environment. All that in mind, it seemed odd that after two weeks of being nearly ineffective, this auditor was discovering all of these issues. We had to audit the auditor.

We discovered that she had gotten access to the system and was booking her own error-filled entries while being logged in as another employee.

When Matt found out, he promptly walked her out the door. That didn't mean that she was simply done with the pilot program and she went back to working in her other GE business. He took her badge and escorted her out of the building. He fired her from GE altogether.

He was true to his word.

KNOW WHEN TO LET GO

So often, leaders hold on to people for too long because they think certain qualities are, in fact, coachable.

Thinking back on my career, when it comes to the spectrum of people I've had to terminate, those individuals tend to occupy one side or the other.

On the one side, I've had people I've gently nudged out.

By that, I mean there are people I've told, "Look, your runway here is not long. You should look for another job." I do that to give them a soft landing. There are people who are typically just not cut out for the job, primarily from a skillset perspective, and there's no other seat for them within the company.

The other end of the spectrum is reserved for those people I'm walking out of the building. You're done. I'm taking your badge, and security is going with us on this stroll.

Invariably, the latter situations occur because of integrity violations.

I once hired a woman as a controller for a company. In the interview, she told me that she wanted to get her MBA and that she wanted the company to support her in that effort. I informed her that it was something we could look into later down the line, but first she needed to come in and do the job, establish herself, and build a good reputation. If she was able to do that, we could revisit the MBA conversation.

She agreed and took the job.

A month in, she approached me again about the MBA. She told me of her plans to apply to a program and asked again for the company's financial support. I reminded her that it had only been a month since we'd first had that conversation and that she needed to stay focused on the job. She was off to a good start, performance-wise, but she still needed to prove herself.

Two months in, she told me she was applying for the MBA whether we were going to support her or not. She understood that it was her money she had to spend, but she was going to do it regardless.

"I've done an executive MBA program," I told her. "You're going to need more than just money. You've got to take time off of work. It's an extra burden on top of what you're doing, and you're just starting off in this job. If this is what you want to do, it's your choice, but I don't think it's your best decision."

Three months later, she came to me and said, "Not only am I doing the MBA, but I want you to pay for it. If you don't, I'm going to leave for a position I've been offered elsewhere."

"Okay," I said. "You should take the job."

"No, no," she said. "I love it here. I love working for you. I'd love to stay and make a commitment."

She hadn't anticipated that I'd call her bluff, but it wasn't just about that. It was about her integrity.

"No," I told her. "You should definitely take that job."

I let HR know immediately that she was exiting and that we were starting a search for a new controller right away.

"Why does it feel like I'm being fired?" she asked.

"You told me that you had another job lined up and that if I didn't give you the financial support you wanted, you were going to leave, so I'm making this easy on you."

She continued with attempts to walk back what she had said, but in my eyes, she had committed an integrity violation. She tried to hold me hostage. That is not the act of someone with integrity.

That is a demonstration of character—something that cannot be coached.

Another time, I inherited a team in which someone was serving as an interim leader for a group but ended up taking the role in a full-time capacity. When I came on board, one of the first orders of business was that the company wanted to promote him to make him the formal full-time leader in his role. He had been second in command and had done a good job in his interim role. I didn't know enough to offer any resistance at that time, so I gave my approval. I figured any issues that might be there would be something I could deal with later.

That was a mistake.

He was not a positive person. He managed up quite well, always telling me what I wanted to hear, but he wasn't managing the team. He let all of the success go to his head and was condescending to his peers or people that were slightly junior to him in position. His promotion had him seeing himself as above them all. He kissed up and kicked down.

There were rumors of happy hours in the office, where he'd have employees do shots. He also used a derogatory term to describe the sexual orientation of a recent hire he had brought in. On top of all of this, his performance in the role had been less than stellar, to say the least. When I finally learned of the toxic culture he had created, I sat him down in a conference room—along with the head of HR and one of the company lawyers.

I shared with him my understanding of what he'd said and done, and the environment he'd created. I made it clear that I had zero tolerance for his behavior, that I found those qualities to be uncoachable. I reiterated my feelings on integrity and that violations like these meant you were no longer with the company.

He shook or nodded his head at the moments he must have thought were appropriate. It was clear he thought I was only giving him feedback.

"You're done today," I told him.

"Wait," he said. "You're firing me?"

The lawyer and head of HR then asked me to leave so they could walk him through the details of his severance package.

Before I did, he asked me to level with him. He wanted to know if he was being fired because he was sleeping with one of his direct reports.

I had been completely unaware that this had been going on, but it proves the old adage true: people will tell you who they are if you let them.

DON'T MAKE THEM FEAR YOU

When you identify someone on your team who has a lack of integrity, you fire them on the spot. You don't say to yourself that you know *someday* it could be a problem. It's a problem today, and this is only the stuff you're aware of. Who knows what else might already be happening that you *don't* know about? As in my previous example, I have seen time and time again when parting ways with someone who demonstrated a lack of integrity that what I saw on the surface was only a fraction of the poor and toxic behavior that individual would engage in.

Matt Marsh set that tone so many years ago. What he did then is why I do what I do now. The first thing I do when I join a new organization as a leader is to set the tone. Part of setting that tone is making sure that I interview every single person that becomes a part of our team. It's something I still do to this day; in fact, I probably spend an average of one day a week doing nothing other than interviewing candidates. I look for the uncoachable traits, and I want candidates to know that if you make it onto the team, I want you to feel comfortable knowing that everyone else I hired onto this team embodies those qualities I seek, and that you can trust these people. You can trust that they have integrity. You can trust that they're positive and team players.

In setting the tone, however, it's important not to establish a culture of fear. I've worked in that environment, too, and it's equally toxic.

Establish that stakes are high, that there are consequences, and that those consequences are severe if lapses that occur involve integrity. There are, of course, consequences for poor performance, but that's why it's also crucial to reward high performance. For example, I tend to be overly generous when it comes to awards. I want my team to know that when they do their jobs well while embodying the traits I hire for, they don't just keep their jobs—there are benefits to be reaped.

Hearing Matt as a leader talk to us, his team, in that way on that night was transformational for me. He embedded in me the seed for the notions that integrity, accountability, collaboration, and positivity were crucial elements for a team, and if someone didn't have them, they could not be coached to develop them. While firing is never an enjoyable task, it was absolutely critical to the team and the company to remove those who were uncoachable.

Knowing and embracing that has served me incredibly well in my leadership journey.

The culture at that company is radically different now. We had people taking shots in the office and making culturally insensitive remarks, and that all stopped. People knew we wouldn't tolerate it. The nonnegotiables had been made crystal clear, and as a result, the company developed an immune system, if you will.

I set the same tone when I joined Axon. Putting the right people in place—and keeping them—has led to better results for the company. Remember those material weaknesses we discussed in the introduction? They're gone. Done and dusted. Our financials are accurate, even if they take us a little longer in terms of closing the books than I'd like. Our investors ask me how I did it. I tell them that I didn't focus on the technical aspects of process improvement, which is what they expect to hear.

I put the right people in place—people I could trust that understood the importance of working on a team—people that I could trust because of the uncoachable qualities they held to get the job done.

NOT ALL FEEDBACK IS GOOD

When communicating with your trustworthy team, it adds to their resiliency if you give them consistent feedback.

However, on my way up the leadership ladder, I learned that not all feedback is good feedback; in fact, some of it can be downright damaging.

Stick with me for this next one. What someone said to me might surprise you.

—

CHAPTER FOUR

"THERE'S SOMETHING WRONG WITH THE WAY YOU LEARN"

In Milwaukee, Matt Marsh, the senior audit manager, had three or four audit managers reporting to him. The rest of the team, including myself, reported to one of these audit managers, whom we'll call Joe.

I was one of a number of auditors working under Joe. Each auditor had their own area to audit during what was called a cycle. One auditor would have revenue recognition, someone else could have inventory, while another might have accounts payable. There were different parts of the balance sheet that we had to audit, and then the audit manager was responsible for some part of the business itself.

During one of our regular meetings to discuss the area I was responsible for, at some point, something was unclear to Joe, so he asked me to explain it in further detail. He took notes, as he usually did, and somewhere in the middle of my explanation, he stopped, and just started listening to me. I found it odd, but I kept going.

Finally, he stopped me and said, "You know something? There's something wrong with the way you learn."

I was taken aback. "What do you mean? Why would you say that?" I said.

"Well," he said, "because I asked someone else to go look into this same thing we're talking about now, and they came back and gave me a very clear answer. It's a pretty simple concept and one you should know by now. You should understand this, and you *clearly* don't."

Dumbstruck. That's the only word I had for how I felt at that moment. I fell all over myself, telling him I'd try to be more concise next time. I walked out of that meeting feeling a bit shell-shocked, trying to figure out what just happened.

For the rest of that audit, Joe seemed to make a habit of taking constant jabs at me—always needling me and trying to get under my skin.

For example, in one meeting, he had pulled our auditor team together for a bit of a pep talk. It was a long audit during the dead of winter in Milwaukee, and everyone was tired and cold. During this time, another auditor had been brought on who was a year behind me and was simply a rock star—just killing it, running circles around everyone. He was finding issues, but the business loved him. Normally, the rest of the team would have felt threatened, but he was such a nice guy, so we all got along well. There were none of the usual cutthroat games I talked about previously.

During this pep talk—and subsequently at pretty much every opportunity he had—Joe would take pains to highlight this new auditor while simultaneously bringing me down. He went around the room telling everyone something he appreciated about them and how much they all made him enjoy the experience.

Then he got to me.

"Jawad, you're like the running back on the team. I'm not going to count on you to make any spectacular plays, but you're always going to punch through two or three yards at a time."

Our relationship was quite contentious from then on.

Despite that, I eventually went on to assume the same position as Joe at the time—I was promoted to become an audit manager.

You get three assignments as an audit manager over the course of one year. By your third assignment, the company decides whether or not they're going to promote you to be a senior auditor based on your performance.

THE GENESIS OF POSITIVITY

My first assignment went...not so great. I was sent to a business in Connecticut that designed all the switch gears and electrical controls for various heavy industries. It was an old-school industrial business—nothing glamorous about it for a young up-and-comer. Almost everyone on my team was older than me, and more than a few of them had some resentment toward me, feeling that I wasn't ready to be a manager. There was noticeable tension. It was my first time managing a team, and I'm certain I wasn't doing things as well as I could have been.

The audit started and I was quickly overwhelmed. As an auditor, I'd been responsible for one area—now I was responsible for all of them. My scope expanded, requiring a great deal of travel, and I had a hard time getting my arms around it. Word moved up to senior management that I was having challenges. My communications to my bosses weren't timely. It was a mess.

Things ended up going so badly that they pulled the plug on my audit. I ended up going from having my own team to being sent on assignments as an auditor working with only one other member of my original team.

That member, Natalia, was actually the genesis behind my idea of making positivity an uncoachable quality. She always had a smile on her face and was always above the fray. She never let it get to her when clients got belligerent with us while we looked for issues. That positivity led her to doing a fantastic job—so much so that I nominated her for one of those cash awards I discussed earlier.

And she won.

Later that night at the ceremony for the award, she found me and said, "I just wanted to thank you. I know this was a tough audit for you, but you were there for me, and this wouldn't have been possible without you."

"Natalia, I didn't do anything. This is all you. From the beginning, you were so positive and upbeat that you wouldn't let any of the nonsense get to you. You stayed intensely focused, and you did it with a smile. I wouldn't have gotten through it without *you*."

She taught me a lesson I wouldn't forget, and I would take it with me.

POSITIVITY

Andrea (also known as AJ, whom you'll meet later in the book) is our head of investor relations (IR) at Axon, and she absolutely embodies positivity.

AJ was the first person I called when the shit hit the fan with the letters from the SEC. She was the one who broke the news to everyone and brought it to our attention. In fact, AJ was so positive that she didn't actually think it was real—that there was no way they could have sent the emails they purported to send!

After the floor fell out from under me and I discovered the emails were in fact in my spam folder, I called to tell her the bad news. She immediately said, "We're going to get through this." She didn't take the time to stew on things or let me wallow. She wanted to focus on all the good things we had done together and the investor day that we had coming up (more on that later), because that was the thing people were really going to focus on—my strategy for the company going forward.

AJ's positivity was a life preserver, not just for me, but for the rest of the team. Even when we screwed up the original messaging to explain what happened with the emails, she didn't let us fall into a hole. There was an "Oh shit" moment when she found out, but she immediately switched gears and moved into action mode.

Additionally, investors *love* her because her positivity is so infectious. Typically, investors only want to meet with the CFO or the CEO. They won't meet with just the head of IR. We send AJ alone to investor conferences, and they are *happy* to have her. This is even more exceptional in a male-dominated field. Her positivity is just one reason that she is a fantastic representative for the team and our company.

My second assignment? I crushed it. As a result, I was told that my performance on the third one would be crucial if I hoped to be promoted. My second assignment, the one I had done well on, was in Dubai. While I was there, I got a call from the company telling me that they wanted me to go to NBC.

Déjà vu all over again.

When I interviewed with them in the beginning of my career, they were just NBC. Between 2003 and 2004, however, GE bought Universal Studios and merged them with NBC to become NBCUniversal, and they wanted me to go to Los Angeles to audit Universal's film business.

My immediate reaction was, "Awesome!" But once again, I had to remind myself not to get starstruck. I had goals and wanted to keep my eye on the prize—getting promoted to senior audit manager. I shared that with them, but they said, "Look, we're putting some heavy hitters on this audit. This is the one where if you nail it, you're going to get promoted."

"Okay, great," I said. "Who's the senior audit manager for that assignment?"

You guessed it. Joe.

My heart sank. Taking an assignment under him again was leaving a *lot* up to chance because Joe made it clear he did *not* like me. Then I remembered how I initially turned down the first GE job offer because I felt slighted when NBC passed on me, and how I came to the realization that feeling of indignation was truly not important.

I decided I'd put what happened with Joe behind me, particularly because I felt I did learn something from him when I worked for him. This was my chance to prove to him that I'd turned things around.

The obstacle was the way.

It was time for me to put this narrative to bed completely.

Not only was I going to do well, I was going to do it with a guy who previously hadn't been my supporter.

Except I get there, and he ends up doing the exact same thing.

Joe gave me a task early on in the audit, just a couple of weeks in. I set my team—because as an audit manager, I now have a team—to the task, and I brought him the results. He looked at what I handed him. Then at me. Then back at what I handed him.

"Look, I want to show you something," he said. He proceeded to pull out a document that another audit manager had put together with his team. "I gave both of you guys the exact same instructions, and look what he came back with. He absolutely crushed it." Then he held up my document. "I don't know what you want me to do with *this*. This is not anything *near* what I was looking for."

I was dumbfounded. "Joe," I said, "you asked me to do something, and I did my best."

"Yeah," he said, "and you didn't get to the right answer."

I struggled throughout that entire audit. I kept trying to give him what he wanted and was never able to do so.

At the end of the audit, when we were up for promotion,

he informed me that he was not going to support me for it. Fortunately, his was not the final say, and I had been told that others were, in fact, recommending me for promotion. I simply told him I appreciated his feedback, but then he said, "Even though I'm not going to support you, some other people are. I want you to know that there's going to be a bit of a discussion about you."

My heart sank. He intimated that not only was he not going to support me but that he was likely going to convince the others to change their minds.

I'll never forget the moment when I got the call. I was in my office in Los Angeles at Universal. My heart was pounding through my chest, because if I made it to my fourth year—even if I didn't make it to my fifth year—the job that I would get coming off as a senior audit manager would make me an executive with the company. When I picked up the phone, the vice president who oversaw the entire audit staff was on the other line.

"Hey, Jawad," he said. "I wanted to let you know that the team had a really long discussion about you. You should know that there were some people that really went to bat for you, but that ultimately, we decided to promote you back into the business."

Being promoted "back into the business" essentially meant

that you were getting booted from the Corporate Audit Staff development program and being asked to find a "regular" job at one of GE's myriad businesses. I wasn't fired, but I wasn't moving up.

I was crushed. It was the first time in a long time that I had failed at something, at least to such a degree that it prevented my upward mobility. More than that, it was the first time that someone told me that although they knew I wanted to go further, I wasn't going to based on their decision. It was incredibly hard to hear, particularly because I felt that maybe with the right coaching, I could have had a great third audit manager assignment, and I was the one who chose to put myself in the situation that I was in.

Afterward, between 2006 and 2010, I found myself alone on an island. When you're in these leadership programs at GE, the company has essentially laid out how your career is going to unfold. You just need to show up and perform.

When you come off that carousel, however, all the music stops. No one is giving you career advice, and no one is giving you feedback on an almost daily basis. You have to fend for yourself like 99 percent of everyone else does. I had been in the middle of this incredibly structured program and now I was on the outside looking in, asking myself, *How do I become relevant again? How am I going to find my way to a position I find meaningful?*

In the midst of that questioning and self-doubt, I moved from role to role, getting feedback from managers that was often inconsistent and conflicting. Because of my previous experience, I was trying to react to that feedback and change my behavior accordingly, but because so much of it was conflicting, it was often difficult to know if, how, and when to act on it, and I became increasingly frustrated.

FILTER VERSUS FUNNEL

People tend to think about feedback in terms of a funnel. They get information from a number of different directions, and they try to hone and synthesize it. I have noted so few people who receive feedback and consider asking others their opinion on it. I see it so clearly now because I was one of those people.

I didn't ask anyone what they thought about Joe's feedback for me. I didn't try to unpack it with anyone to see if it was even accurate. I did what so many of us do—I internalized it. I never stopped to think that maybe this feedback wasn't worth listening to in the first place. If there were others in the company that were going to bat for me when Joe wasn't, clearly I had been doing something right, yet I wasn't able to filter out his feedback.

In fact, I had internalized it so deeply that I began to worry that there was actually something wrong with my brain and the way I learned. I began to question whether or not I needed to see a therapist or to get my IQ tested. It made me question myself and all the things I had done to get to where I was at that point. There's no question that it affected my performance moving forward.

One of the reasons I'm in the seat I am today and have had the success I've had is because I learned how to have confidence. I have an incredible team around me because they find inspiration in my confidence, and they trust that I will lead them in the right direction, but I didn't always have that, and it certainly didn't come overnight. That period of time on that audit and after missing that promotion was one of serious self-doubt—to the extent that I thought I might truly have a learning disability.

Developing a filter for feedback is crucial if you want to be an effective, confident leader. Feedback is useful in terms of fine-tuning your trajectory—it should be utilized to make course corrections. You shouldn't simply go left or go right based on where people are telling you to go.

Developing that filter for myself has drastically changed the way I *give* feedback to the people I am leading.

Before I sit someone down to discuss my observations of their work and behavior, the first question I ask myself is: *Will this be something that is actionable for this person?*

If it's not, I keep my mouth shut. Why would I introduce something like that when it only serves to seed self-doubt? It's hard enough for people to navigate their careers as it is. Why would I add to that a stress I myself have already experienced?

When you give feedback, not only should it be actionable, but it should include some form of recommendation for how they can improve. For example, if a team member gives me a presentation on a spreadsheet that's twenty tabs deep, I'm going to ask them to go back and synthesize that information in a way that's more accessible and digestible so that I and others can see at a glance what the most important takeaway is. Telling them it sucks and to fix it is neither helpful nor actionable, particularly if they felt that first effort was their best.

If you're not already doing this as a leader, don't assume it's easy to simply switch gears. Just as I didn't develop confidence overnight, neither did I immediately give feedback in the best ways.

In my first assignment as an audit manager, one woman who worked for me was from India. She had a habit of talking continually until she was interrupted. In our one-on-ones, I would ask her a question, and her answers would continue on and on until I had to stop her just to get a word in.

"Look, you're actually bringing up some really good points," I said, "but they're getting lost in this stream of verbal diarrhea. Just try to distill what you're saying to a really concise message."

Smooth, right?

Of course, she didn't know what to do with that, particularly because she was accustomed to adding filler words and being verbose. It got to the point where I was stopping her where I thought the sentence should end, then asking another question, then stopping her again, like she was a child. I can only imagine how embarrassing it must have been for her. Had I known then what I know now, I would have given her recommendations about how to improve for future communications and let her work on it on her own instead of condescending to her and forcing her to change mid-conversation.

LEAD BY EXAMPLE

With any failure, though, you have the opportunity to learn how to get it right, and those you lead stand to learn from it when they are leaders themselves.

For example, one of the managers on my team, AJ, is responsible for a team of her own, but when she came to me, she had never managed a large team of people before. She had assigned someone to manage an email inbox where important emails from investors who own a large number of shares in the company came in. There was lot on the line if those emails went unread.

AJ had caught this employee once not watching the inbox carefully, and then it happened again, and this time, some extremely important messages slipped through the cracks. Luckily, nothing occurred that couldn't be salvaged, but it was clear to AJ that she had to communicate more effectively to this team member the importance of diligently monitoring the emails.

All through AJ's career, she'd been negatively managed, and so in turn, that's the kind of manager she was in this instance. She shared with this employee all the dire consequences of dropping the ball again. She informed him that they could miss a shareholder vote because he missed an email, and the results of that could be the loss of his job.

She learned quickly that feedback based on fear is never an effective motivator. Instead of inspiring this team member to do a great job, all AJ managed to do was upset him and make him fear for his job. He felt as though he couldn't perform and wanted to quit because the stage had been set for him to be let go. He felt that if the consequences were indeed so terrible, he shouldn't be in charge of that task.

AJ brought me this story, and I told her what she had done wrong in delivering her feedback, but even then, AJ gave some resistance.

She said, "Well, it's not my fault he's upset. He needs to know that he needs to do his job."

Then AJ sat with what I said and went back to her team member and spent time with him, going through why it was so critical that this special inbox was so closely watched. She taught him about the different types of investors and more generally brought him into that world and worked to motivate him with the positive vision that as a team, we're highly responsive, we take care of things, and most importantly, that he was capable of doing this important job. She still communicated a sense of urgency, but she did it in a way that was uplifting and inspirational.

AJ told me that she managed that team member the way I managed her, and it led to success for them both. In fact, AJ was able to apply it to her own communication skills.

When she first started with the company, AJ was having some logistical challenges. She was breastfeeding her baby at the time and had to travel with her child and her au pair. In a meeting with our CEO where we were coordinating meetings and travel plans, she went into a bit of overshare.

She told me later that it was because she wanted people to understand what she was dealing with.

Even though she felt she was being open and transparent, she in fact confused people with an unclear message. I communicated with her that instead of defending her actions, she should just offer a firm yes or no as to whether or not she could be at a certain location at a certain time and know that I would have her back to support whatever she needed to do from a personal standpoint.

She saw the lack of clarity immediately and began implementing a new approach—so much so that she told me she noticed other people doing it to her in her life and gave them the same advice. Because my feedback to her was positive and actionable, she was able to do something with it that served her and the team.

NOT ONE SIZE FITS ALL

It's important to remember that feedback, depending on the person, can cut deep, even if it's delivered in a positive and actionable manner. People don't like to hear they haven't done something well, particularly when they believe they've put their best foot forward. The way we see the world is often ingrained in us. When we receive input about our performance that doesn't fit our worldview, it can throw us for a loop that may even result in some spin-out. It can take a while for that feedback to sink in, if it does at all.

There is a young woman, Angel, on my team who is in an investor relations role, working under AJ. Angel started out as my admin, and prior to that, she was a licensed beautician. However, from the day I first interviewed her, I saw in her so many of the uncoachable traits that make an incredible team member that I had to bring her on board and find ways to give her more responsibility.

AJ, however, gave orders and feedback to Angel like she was any other analyst from Wall Street—people who were used to a direct, sometimes blunt, delivery. Angel didn't come from that world—not even close. Unsure of herself, Angel wondered if she even belonged here. She didn't have AJ's education or opportunities; she was in the role because she had qualities that couldn't be trained. AJ didn't tailor her feedback to Angel's unique experience. It wasn't that AJ's feedback was incorrect, but the way in which she gave it was.

THE STORY OF ANGEL

Angel worked for one of my direct reports as an office manager when I was working in Chicago. Prior to that, she had begun school with the aim of being a pediatrician, but quickly discovered it was not her path. The problem was she didn't know what her path actually was. Her friends talked her into going to beauty school, and she earned her license as a beautician. Before too long, however, she found she still wasn't getting the job satisfaction she sought, though she discovered that she had a real gift in working with people, largely due to her overwhelming *positivity*. It was then that she took the office manager position at my office in Chicago.

Already at that time, I had observed her *accountability*, as she often came to me for advice as to how to do her job. In one of our conversations, she mentioned that she and her boyfriend were looking to leave Chicago. Not long after that, I had accepted the position at Axon (then TASER) in Arizona. She jokingly told me to call her if I ever had an opening once I was there.

I asked her to become my executive administrator, and it was one of the best decisions I had made, both for myself and for the company.

Other functions in the company quickly gleaned that Angel was a *collaborative* rock star—so much so that after recruiting her to work on events and other various tasks in their departments, they tried to hire her away from me.

She ended up helping AJ with some of our investor relations events. She instilled such trust in AJ and everyone on her team with her unflappable *integrity* and desire to do right by people, along with all of the other qualities we mentioned, that she serves solely in that function today, working directly with AJ as an IR analyst, participating in high-level investor calls and meetings. In fact, Angel has advanced so rapidly and built so much trust that we sometimes have her take calls with investors by herself, and we get great feedback on her performance.

Her possession of those uncoachable qualities led to a meteoric rise for her career, and she's just getting started.

Remember that even when you're giving positive and actionable feedback, you have to consider the person as a whole. Not all feedback can be delivered in the same way and be effective for everyone. There are personality considerations. There are cultural considerations. You cannot give someone *effective* feedback unless you understand, to some extent, their view of themselves. Otherwise, you're simply sharing lessons you've learned that will ultimately have no impact on that person because it doesn't resonate with their experience. As a leader, you have to consider the effect your delivery has as a person who is perceived to be in a position of power, no matter how much you are there to be a servant leader for your team.

That perception is powerful because as we've so often heard, perception is reality for the individual.

We're going to talk about why that's such an important consideration for you as a leader and your team in the next chapter.

CHAPTER FIVE

———

"I'M SO HAPPY FOR YOU, BUT I'M PUTTING YOU ON A PIP"

I learned a lot about the power of feedback, but not immediately.

In 2009, I worked in Ireland for GE's aircraft leasing business, in that period when I was trying to work myself back up to a point where I could get noticed and, eventually, promoted. I was brought over to work in that business by one of my first bosses, Jamey Mock, who is today the CFO for PerkinElmer, a large multinational healthcare company. Jamey knew my work and he trusted me, and in turn, I'd run through walls for him as I would for Matt Marsh.

I worked for Jamey on the Corporate Audit Staff. Jamey recruited me to the aircraft leasing business, thinking he'd be there for a while and would help me get promoted, but he was also a rock star at GE and quickly got tapped for a bigger role himself back at GE's aircraft engines business in Cincinnati. I was in Ireland when Jamey got the call, and by the time I got back to the United States, I had a new boss. When I told her about what Jamey had in store for me, she had no interest in it—she wanted to build her own team that was loyal to her.

In Jamey's place came a supervisor who did not share his level of trust in me, to put it charitably.

As such—to be blunt—I made myself a thorn in her side.

The truth is that I still had a lot of growing up to do from a professional perspective. Maybe I still felt stung by being passed over for the promotion; maybe I was hurt that my old boss had exited. Either way, there was no excuse for my behavior.

I publicly disagreed with her in meetings. I'd tell her I didn't think she was taking the right course of action or would disagree with her conclusions. I was purposely being an ass because I thought I was asserting myself. I wanted to project a confidence that I hadn't necessarily earned at that point. She also made a point of telling me that all the goodwill and political capital I had earned with my previous supervisor had essentially been wiped clean. Here I was, a breath away from the promotion I'd fallen short on, and she told me I wasn't even in sniffing distance of being an executive. That was exceedingly tough for me to hear, so I went into reaction mode.

And it bit me in the ass.

On my last day of work before I was to leave for my wedding, she messaged me and said, "Hey, can you stop by my office on your way out?" and then asked me to do another task that was going to delay my getting out the door. I was already frustrated with her, and that she would do this as I was preparing to leave for one of the most important events in my life really amped me up. Still, I did what I was tasked with and stopped by her office. I assumed that she just wanted to review the task, but we went through that rather quickly.

"There's one other thing I'd like to talk to you about," she said.

"Fine," I said.

"I'm just going to say it. It's been really difficult working with you, and I need you to turn things around. I need you to change your attitude toward how you're approaching your job. If you don't, when you return, I'm putting you on a performance improvement plan."

"What?" I said.

"Don't misunderstand; I'm really happy for you," she said. "I know with this wedding and everything that you've got some really good things you're looking forward to. Seriously, congratulations. But I'm putting you on a PIP when you get back if I don't see some changes."

"Okay," I said, seething. "Are you done?"

She said yes, and I stormed out of her office.

IT DIDN'T MATTER WHAT I THOUGHT

The entire plane ride to Florida, I was fuming. What right did she have to say that to me right before I was getting married? Who did she think she was? I started asking some of my friends and colleagues about it. I'm not the type to keep things bottled up. I like to share and socialize and get other people's input—although, if I'm being honest, it was much more likely that I was doing it to validate my anger.

Then one of those people started to ask me questions—

questions like "Why do you think she has this view of you?" I started thinking about all of the things that got me to that moment in her office, and it made me realize something.

It didn't matter what I thought.

It didn't matter how right I thought I was or how good I thought I was or what trajectory I was on. What mattered is that my direct boss felt like I was a pain in her ass—so much so that she was ready to deviate my career, if not drum me out of the company altogether.

Her perception was her reality, and her reality, like it or not, was mine too.

Instead of doubling down on it and getting even more frustrated, I decided to push all of that out the window. Yes, there were times when I felt she micromanaged me. Yes, there were times when she said things that I found somewhat degrading. Yet when I returned, I didn't let any of that matter. I stopped pushing back and was resolute that I was all about making her happy.

"I'LL ABSOLUTELY SUPPORT YOU"

A year passed and an opportunity arose—a big one. I had the opportunity to take a CFO role.

GE was doing an organic startup, something they didn't typically do often—they usually entered new spaces via an acquisition. This time, however, they decided to spin up a completely new company from scratch, and they had put in a leader to run it, a GM for the business. They needed a CFO, and because the business was fairly small, the role would be too, so they were looking for a first-timer in the position.

A friend within the company who had often been a sounding board for me recommended me strongly for the role, but before you interview for another job in the company, you have to ask your boss if you can.

You can imagine the nerves before I went into her office.

I laid out all the reasons this would be good for me. A CFO role was everything I'd wanted. It was going to be back home in Boston, which would put me closer to my parents. It felt like the stars were aligned.

"I would love to take a chance at this," I told her.

She folded her hands in front of her on her desk. I braced for the bad news.

"If you had asked me a year ago, I would have said, 'No way.'"

I swallowed hard.

"However," she said, "you've totally turned things around,
I mean a complete 180. If this is what you want to do, I'll
absolutely support you."

I almost jumped out of my chair. I interviewed and
was offered the role. I accepted, and it was the job that
launched my career into orbit.

DEFINING YOUR NORTH STAR

In the year between getting married and landing my first CFO gig, I
did more than eat crow. I defined, for the first time in my career, my
North Star.

As I reflected on my situation at the time, I realized that I was basically
jumping from job to job, waiting to get tapped on the shoulder for my
next role. What dawned on me was that if I kept doing that, I'd end
up where other people wanted me to be, and not necessarily where
I wanted to be. So I took some time to think about what it was that I
wanted to do, and what I kept coming back to was I wanted to do it all.
I wanted to run my own company.

Finance is a great career, but I didn't want to be pigeonholed as a
"finance guy." Thinking back to how I picked my economics major in
college, what I loved about work was rolling up my sleeves and getting
deep into the details of a business and then seeing how that eventually

manifested in positive business results. I wanted to do that on a much larger scale, with a much greater span of control over an organization.

I then worked backward from there. I looked at the careers of CEOs and business leaders that I admired and studied what paths they took to get to where they were. I saw lots of founder/CEOs, but I also saw lots of functional heads, such as sales, operations, and—you guessed it—finance. Thinking that it would take too long to go learn a skill I could master enough to start my own company, I decided my best path forward was to get to the top of my function. My next step backward from CEO was therefore to become a CFO.

Before becoming CFO of an entire company, I wanted to first try my hand at being CFO of a division of a large company such as GE. I was ambitious but wanted to walk before I could run.

I had also decided that I was done making lateral moves. I made a lateral move coming over to work for the aircraft leasing business, thinking that Jamey would help me get to the next level. When he left, I found myself without a network of supporters, and the prospects of the promotion that had been dangled in front of me evaporated.

Despite being approached by recruiters for jobs that would have paid more and gotten me out of a situation I wasn't thrilled to be in, I decided to grit it out and wait for the right opportunity that would keep me advancing toward my North Star. As you'll soon see, it wasn't the last time I would do that, and it would transform my career.

Today, I don't feel as much of a need to keep chasing my North Star because it feels in many ways as if I've already arrived there. I'm extremely fortunate to be in my current situation. I own several functions at Axon besides finance. I don't need the CEO title. Our executive team is very tight-knit, and we're all running the business together, which is really what I wanted. In fact, I couldn't ask for a better boss than Rick, a transformative and inspirational leader who is changing the world with his vision for bringing advanced technologies to law enforcement.

None of this would have become reality if I hadn't defined my North Star all those years ago and relentlessly pursued it.

PERCEPTION *IS* REALITY

It sounds cliché to say, but it's true.

The two weeks I spent in Florida after my supervisor told me she'd put me on a PIP gave me time to cool down and think. I came to the realization that I had to step away from this situation and attempt to think about it objectively. In doing so, I realized that, for starters, I really had been a bit of an ass—that much was clear—but even if I hadn't, it was also clear to me that it didn't matter. How she saw me was her reality, and because she was my supervisor, that was what mattered in the end.

That experience served me in my career in more ways than just getting the job I wanted. From that moment on,

I made a point of taking the time to reflect on situations that weren't entirely positive and tried to be introspective about them. Those moments often led to realizations that changed my mind frame about them, sometimes in transformative ways.

In fact, this instance with the PIP took me back to the employee who was asking me about supporting her for the MBA. The truth was she was very good at her job, and she knew it. The shoe was on the other foot. Looking back on my situation, I understood from a better perspective how my boss felt because it was how I felt when that employee did essentially the same thing to me.

HOW DO PEOPLE VIEW YOU?

I tell my direct reports when they're managing their own teams that it's vitally important for them to consider and understand how people view them.

You might think you're the best leader on the planet, but if your teams are unresponsive, or people are quitting, or they're unhappy about their pay, something is going on. In general, your team should be happy. If they're not, it's important to turn your search inward first.

If you don't? The resultant problems will manifest themselves at the worst possible time—when you need your teams the most.

I see myself as more of an advisor than a manager, and it's how I coach my teams to behave when they're leading people. Only when you're an advisor can you really empower your teams to spread their wings and succeed or fail but—more importantly—learn. However, being an advisor can only happen when your team is full of people that you trust, who are competent and happy. If they are not even one of those things, then you really can't advise them. Then you become a manager.

ACCOUNTABILITY

Isaiah was the number two to the general counsel (who also happened to be the former president of TASER, had been with the company for the better part of two decades, and was a beloved figure in the company). When the general counsel transitioned into retirement, Isaiah served in the position provisionally and had some huge shoes to fill.

In fact, after the general counsel announced his retirement, Isaiah was provisional for almost a year. The previous general counsel was a section 16 officer (a named officer in the company) whose compensation was public, stock trades were public, etc. This also put him into another level of compensation. Yet when Isaiah was made general counsel, he was not made a section 16 officer.

Isaiah could have been annoyed about this and let it affect his account-ability, but he works as hard today as he did when he was in the number two spot, where he was essentially trying out for his job. His attitude and approach never changed. He's constantly meeting with customers, going to product trials, and going to DC to represent us. He possesses a *huge* sense of accountability.

The legal function is one of the strongest in the company, and it's because of him. He was in provisional status during the SEC issue, and he worked it as though he'd been the general counsel forever. He stepped up and took ownership of everything without ever being asked. In fact, we could have gone back to his predecessor and asked for his help when the SEC problems hit, but Isaiah insisted on owning it. He kept the previous general counsel involved, but he took the bull by the horns.

Isaiah isn't afraid to seek advice from others. I've seen him, on numerous occasions, speak to other law firms to gain their perspectives and opinions on certain legal issues. He is without ego, and this allows him to look at everything with a 360-degree view and bring fully informed advice to the management and executive teams.

While he has this unflappable, unemotional response to crises, there is a physical change in Isaiah when something bad happens, even when he has no fault in it. He takes it so hard because he has such an intense sense of ownership. During the SEC issue, he went out of his way to share some of the emotional load and help me out.

Being accountable for your own area is table stakes—Isaiah has that accountability for the entire company. Because he's so accountable, he requires the least "management" of almost anyone in the company. His accountability makes him eminently credible and reliable. I know I can count on him to get the job done.

SUCCESS AND EXPERIENCE EQUALS CREDIBILITY

As you move into bigger and bigger roles, the perception your team and other people have of you is not just based on what you do at your desk from day to day. It also comes from the success you're having.

In my current role, I'm responsible for giving CFO updates to our board of directors every quarter. I go through a number of slides and give an update on the business, including, of course, our financials. In one of my early updates, I talked about how we had remediated our earlier material weaknesses, how we upgraded our accounting team, and how we recently hired some terrific talent, including a new head of Corporate Strategy.

When I do these presentations, I go big. I put a ton of work into preparing a PowerPoint deck, something I mastered at GE, even when a simple written update would suffice. I wear a suit or sports coat, even though I don't have to. These things are important because, again, perception is reality. I want our board to see me as a supercompetent

CFO and see that in person. They hear about the great team I'm building; they see how the stock price has gone up during my tenure. I want them to feel fortunate to have me as a member of the team and feel confident in the work that I'm doing.

Having that credibility allows me, quite simply, to get things done. If our CEO wants to move forward with an initiative that I don't feel is in the company's best financial interest at the time, I have his ear to tell him that, and because he believes in me, he listens. If I need to increase the size of my team in a way that exceeds my current budget, but I can project how those additions will make the company money in the long run, I have that freedom.

Your perception is not just about your individual performance with your team—it's also about your track record of success. It is your reality in the moment, but it's also about what you've been able to accomplish.

SEE IT FROM THEIR SIDE

Embracing the idea that perception is reality helps you to understand your team members better.

As I mentioned, when the employee who wanted the MBA put me in the position that she did, I had an epiphany of sorts about what it must have been like for the manager who wanted to put me on a PIP. I realized what a nuisance I had been to her and how I had undermined her efforts.

In retrospect, the experience also made me more sympathetic to other employees—even for the one pushing for the support of her MBA (at first). When I encounter similar situations now, I have to tell myself that the person in question is acting out for some reason that might not be immediately apparent to me. That person has people they care about, and they might be going home and talking to those people the same way I was when I was at the peak of my frustration.

The question for me then becomes: What can I do to give this employee a better experience?

It might not always be compensation. Sometimes it can be giving them time off. Recognition in front of their peers. Opportunities to have their opinions heard in front of leadership. There is a litany of things that you can do to make that person feel as though they are in the boat with you, helping to steer, instead of just having orders barked at them by the captain.

ASK YOUR TEAM FOR FEEDBACK

I am constantly asking my team for feedback. It's critical to understanding how they perceive me.

We have regularly scheduled all-hands meetings where I get up in front of the entire company to deliver an update. Anytime I do those—or anytime I'm presenting anything in front of a group of people—I always ask between three and five people how they feel I did. What could I have done differently? How did they feel it was received?

I'm here to tell you that I don't always get the answer I'd like to hear.

We have an affinity group called the Women at Axon. At one of their meetings, they held a diversity roundtable and invited me to come speak. When I did, I made the case that I had seen men advocating for themselves all the time, whether it be for promotions or salary increases, and how I would love to see more women do the same—that they had just as much right to speak up for themselves. I related how men in the company were constantly coming to me advocating for themselves, but with women, it almost never happened.

I made this point in the context of having personally seen a number of incompetent men in leadership positions over the course of my career. When you see a woman in a leadership position, she has usually overcome a great deal to get there, and I've yet to meet a single female executive that was even borderline incompetent. I was of the opinion that men can fake their way into that sort of thing where women largely cannot.

Later, I asked one of the leaders of the group for her feedback.

She said, "Since you're asking, I'll tell you that it came across as though you were telling women to act more like men."

I was stunned because it wasn't the message I intended to deliver *at all*. Concerned, I asked another member of the group, and they, too, had gotten that impression. While a large number of others in the group had not, it was another reminder for me that what I perceive and what others perceive can be vastly different and that the importance of feedback regarding that perception cannot be ignored.

PERCEPTION AND MINORITIES

We have a loose culture at Axon. This company feels like home to me, so I can be who I am here, which means I can dress in the comfortable way I like.

Not everyone can do that, especially if you are a minority.

If you are part of a marginalized community and don't

have the privilege of working in a company culture like Axon, you're going to have to play the game to some degree. I learned that as part of my journey to a place where I no longer have to do that.

If your workplace is business casual, dress just a notch above that. If you have the ability to work from home, but your boss is big on face time in the office, I suggest you're the first one in the building in the morning and the last to leave at the end of the day. If you're permanently working from home in this postcoronavirus world, it's even more critical that you're proactively reaching out to your boss or other supporters in your organization. Don't have meetings just to have them, but even a brief fifteen-minute video conference call updating them on what you're working on will keep you top of mind. Like it or not, the old adage is true, because it speaks to human nature—out of sight, out of mind.

Whether you want to believe it or not and whether or not it's fair—it isn't—the perceptions some have about you were formed before you ever opened your mouth. That's to say nothing about what they became once you actually *did* speak.

Ask me how I know.

Those perceptions have always been there about me, and

I would not let someone else's narrative dictate my trajectory. I was the first one in and last one out. I dressed well when I wasn't required to do so. I took online lessons in diction and enunciation, voice projection, and body language, including how to use my hands during public speaking. I learned what plays in an executive conference room or with investors. Me coming in and putting my feet up on the table while we spitball ideas wasn't going to fly with them.

Not when it's me.

If you are a person from a marginalized community with leadership aspirations, you must be even more alert, even more cognizant to the fact that you have an extra layer of perception to manage before you even open your mouth.

It's also important to understand that if you are a leader who is not from one of these communities, the workforce is becoming increasingly more diverse and will continue to do so. If you are an affluent white male in a position of power, it is *critical* that you realize that not everyone has had the same experiences you have—that it is highly likely that they did not have the same path you did.

You cannot tell people there is something wrong with the way they learn because you have no idea how they learn. This ties back into feedback, but it's also a crucial element of perception. While it is going to be difficult for you to understand their experiences, you must not allow your perceptions, in this case, to become your reality because in this case, your reality is not theirs. Recognizing this is vital to your mutual respect for each other, as well as your successes, and that of your company.

TIME TO STEP UP

With a powerful lesson in my toolbox, it was time for me to move up to the position I had worked so hard for. I was ready to take on my first CFO position.

Or was I?

CHAPTER SIX

"I NEED YOU TO
BE THE HEAVY"

Taking that CFO role at GE meant moving back to Boston, where this new division was headquartered.

The general manager for the business, Earl Jones, the man who hired me, is someone who I keep in touch with to this very day. He was easily one of the most influential people I've ever worked for. He was a former nuclear submarine commander, with a master's in electrical engineering and an MBA, both from MIT. That is to say he's incredibly smart and a natural-born leader. I learned an immense amount from him. As I mentioned in the previous chapter, the time I spent with him in this role was transformative for me, as I've now been a CFO for the last decade.

But the transition to the role was not easy.

THERE IS A CERTAIN WAY TO THE WORLD

My mother worked for the company Raytheon for over thirty years. For those unfamiliar, Raytheon is a defense company, one of the largest in the world. They make radars and missiles, most notably the Patriot missile, which came to prominence during the first Gulf War. In fact, my mother worked on the Patriot missile program. Raytheon even put out baseball cards that had all their different products on them. My mother brought them home, and I collected them because as a twelve-year-old, I was fascinated by the whole war machine concept.

Former President George H. W. Bush visited Raytheon, and I had the opportunity to meet him. Afterward, I told my mother that I wanted to be president someday too.

"You're never going to be president," she said.

I didn't understand.

"I want to support you in whatever it is that you want to do," she continued, "but I want you to be realistic. You're brown and you're Muslim. You're not going to be president."

My mother is and has always been incredibly supportive

of me, but she wanted me to understand very early on that there was a certain way to the world, and the sooner I learned to accept that, the better off I'd be.

From that moment on, I assumed that that's the way it was, and that was how it was going to be. It didn't help that for part of my life, I didn't talk like everyone else because my parents both had accents, and so when I was young, I spoke with an accent too, and kids made fun of me for it. I was a chubby kid growing up and tall for my age, and the kids ridiculed me for that as well. Not only that, but I was of a different faith than most of them. All of this fed into my view of myself and what I could and could not do.

Fast-forward to 2010, back to Boston in my first CFO role.

While I won't say I was timid going into the role, based on my assumptions about the way the world worked, I didn't understand that I could assert myself in a certain way.

"TELL THEM TO FUCK OFF AND DIE"

This new business was a part of GE Healthcare's IT business. There were three companies in this IT space. One was Electronic Medical Records; one was imaging software for CAT scans, MRIs, and other medical devices; and the third was our business, which largely focused on health information exchange software that connected the various systems at a hospital.

The first two were $500-million to $600-million businesses, where ours was at approximately $20 million, which is to say we were the smallest of the three. We had just started up and had a bit of an underdog mentality. We knew we were going to grow as big as the others, but we weren't there yet by a longshot. This was Earl's second general manager role and my first CFO role. He had assembled a good team, but we were still seen as the little brother to these bigger businesses.

One day, I took a call from a CFO from one of the bigger divisions. He told me that there was a charge they had that they were going to transfer to us as an expense we all could share for some software asset we were all using. He wanted to spread it evenly and split it three ways.

When I took it to Earl, he wasn't having it.

"Tell them it should be based on revenue," he told me. "They should eat far more of the expense than us."

I did as I was told. The business responded, predictably, that this decision was not based on revenue or usage and that we were going to take the expense on as an equal three-way split.

I took their answer back to Earl. He sat back in his chair and looked out the window to his office.

"Here's what I want you to do. I want you to call them back and tell them to fuck off."

He paused, and I held my breath, my mouth gaping.

"No, wait. I want you to tell them to fuck off and die," he said.

I exhaled with a laugh.

He wasn't amused. He sat forward at his desk. "Don't come into my office and report the weather. I need you to take ownership of our P&L [profit and loss, or income statement] and drive outcomes."

I wasn't laughing anymore.

"Jawad, listen to me," he said. "I need you to be the heavy. I've been the leader of both military and nonmilitary organizations, and I know what's effective. I have to be viewed as inspirational. People look to me for that. I can't be both inspirational *and* the heavy. It doesn't work that way."

"Okay," I said, "but I don't command the same respect you do." I could hear my mother's words echoing in my ears.

"You're smart, Jawad," he said. "You know what we need to do. Tell people what to do and they will listen to you. If they don't, I'll always have your back. Be confident in that."

And he did have my back. His actions proved him to be true to his word and not just in that instance.

So did I go back and tell the other business to fuck off and die?

Kind of.

The CFO of the bigger division wasn't my boss—that was the group CFO. I didn't tell my peer to fuck off, but I did escalate the issue to my boss, and we all had a discussion about it. My argument was that from his level (the group CFO), it was the same expense no matter how it was split, so why not just allocate it based on revenues?

He agreed with me. It was one of the first times I realized, *Hold on a second here—it's okay for me to push back as long as I'm making a sound and logical argument.*

It's something I still do to this day. When I disagree with someone, I mentally list out the reasons for my argument and consider counterpoints and then come up with my own counterpoints for those. Then I go hard to the paint on arguing those, not on puffing my chest. Even if the other person doesn't capitulate, I still end up influencing the outcome.

It's one thing to do this when you disagree with one other person, but I've done this even when I'm alone among a group that doesn't agree with me, including my boss. When that happens, you not only have to build your case, you also need to build a coalition and slowly win supporters to your side behind the scenes. Then when it comes time to have an actual meeting where you decide the issue, you've already done the work ahead of time, and the people still standing against you (who are hopefully in the minority at this point) don't see it coming.

This is much more effective than telling someone to fuck off.

When our division began budget planning for the next year, everyone came in with an ask that was more than what Earl and I had told them they could have. Because I had not been viewed as a heavy at that point, they thought they'd all get away with it. I had always been viewed, even in previous jobs, as too nice. I didn't have enough of an edge. I couldn't have the tough discussions. Short of swearing and acting belligerent, I didn't know how to act when the situation called for a strong stance. As promised, Earl stepped in.

"Jawad," Earl said, "what's your call here?"

"No," I said. "We have to stick to our budget. We made a commitment to each other and to the GE division investing in us, and we have to honor it."

"All right, then," he said. "You heard the man."

After some time, people learned to listen to me. They stopped trying to work around me because they knew Earl would support me. It was so empowering and effective. It removed my timidity and allowed me to lead in a more confident and efficient manner. I no longer worried about what other people would say. I could be the heavy not just because Earl supported me but because that support unlocked the confidence I needed to do so.

It also allowed me to experiment with honing a little bit of that edge by engaging in those tough discussions I'd previously avoided. I could see how far I could go with it. I could stretch people beyond what they thought was their comfort zone with me. Doing so, I found the perfect middle ground that allowed me to be direct with people without being over the top. I set clear expectations, including that I expected my expectations to be honored.

I discovered through this process that people, for the most part, *want* to be led. It's human nature. This is not to say that they want to be told what to do, but they do want to be given direction. When you give that direction and you're confident in it—when you can articulate the reason why—people will follow. If you can make them feel as though they are a part of whatever decision you're asking them to follow, then they'll be even more willing to do so.

In my role as CFO at Axon, that empowerment that I received served me well.

I had a call with an investor from one of the largest asset managers in the country. They had been looking to take a position in our stock. On a recent earnings call, we had to report that we had missed the target on our revenue.

The typical move when this occurs is to lower the guidance for the year. I decided that we were going to keep it where it was because as I analyzed the rest of the year, I saw we had a shot at hitting it. I decided that I didn't want to let my team off the hook by lowering it. We were going to leave it and fight like hell to get back there. Wall Street did not like that idea. They didn't see any way for us to accomplish that, and thought that not only was I shooting a hole in my credibility, I was introducing even greater risk.

This investor began taking me to task on the phone call, repeating the Wall Street sentiment, and I cut him off.

"I disagree," I said. "There's no more inherent risk in the business. Operationally, there are things we need to do to get to these revenue and margin targets, and they are all things within our control. My changing the guidance doesn't change whether or not we deliver on these things. I disagree with your assertion that we're introducing more risk. I have to manage the business based on the facts in front of me. I can't have the guidance reflect investor paranoia."

The line went quiet. He was used to CFOs asking how high when he said jump. Then he said, "Time is going to prove one of us right. I hope for your sake, it's you."

Had Earl not empowered me in my time at GE, and had my current CEO and I not established a similar rapport, I never would have had the courage to do that.

DRIVE BEHAVIORS AND OUTCOMES

Driving behaviors and outcomes is an extension of the choice you make to become a leader.

So how do you do it? How do you effect change?

You have to have the difficult discussions with people. You cannot expect your team to follow you if you're not that person.

For example, had I rolled over for the investor on that call, there would have been a ripple effect for my team. They were a demanding investor and doing what they asked would have given them more and more of my time, and they would, in many ways, expect me to be subservient to them. That's not me, and that is not my team.

In fact, AJ, whom I've referenced before, was on that initial call. Her initial instinct was to kowtow to him, as he represented such a large institutional investor, but she later said, "I thought about what you said to him, and you were right. We shouldn't bend over backward for him. That's not who we are as a company."

I effectively played the heavy—in a somewhat different way—with the investor, and it worked to inspire my team. That decision to hold steady on the guidance will drive their behavior and outcomes to make sure we hit that mark, specifically because I said that my team was capable—that we would not bow down to paranoia.

ONE OF US WAS RIGHT

Companies give guidance in different ways. Some will give public guidance. For example, Apple will give their guidance based on revenue or on the number of iPhones that will be shipped in a quarter. A company like Tesla might give their guidance based on costs.

At Axon, we decided that for 2019, we were going to guide based on two things—revenue and EBITDA (earnings before interest, tax, depreciation, and amortization), which is a measure of profitability. We told investors, "We're going to give you the top-line revenue and the bottom-line profit, and that's it." In this case, it was $480 million to $490 million in revenue and $80 million to $85 million in EBITDA.

The problem in 2019 was that in our second quarter, we had a miss on our revenue, and the investors lost all confidence that we would hit our profit number. That's why the one investor in this particular case was so upset that we didn't change our revenue guidance number. They felt that even the low end would be tough for us, if not impossible.

As I said, I didn't want to let the team off the hook. We needed to rally around this goal we had set for ourselves. We needed to take a collective stand. If we didn't, one miss in a quarter could have become two. That was unacceptable for us.

I'm happy and proud to report that we came in at $531 million in revenue and $88 million in profitability, blowing our projected guidance out of the water.

The best part is that we were able to turn around and reinvest that money back in the company, specifically research and development to create an even better product to further the company's mission and further drive our profitability. Hitting those numbers allowed us to execute on initiatives that might not have been possible without that level of profitability.

As a leader, it is important for you to serve those who manage your teams in this way as well. You must support their decision such that they feel empowered, but you must also let them know that they can't act as weather reporters. They can't just come and tell you what's going on. You need them to drive change, behaviors, and outcomes as well. There are always going to be people who push back against their initiatives, but it is their job to make sure that everyone stays on track.

GET TO THE RIGHT ANSWER

When discussing how to lead, there are three ideas I always stand by.

Work hard, do the right thing, and get to the right answer. The first two are relatively easy. It's tough to get to the right answer because in order to do that, you have to be very self-aware, and you have to have the humility to admit when you're wrong. It's not enough to give people direction and know that someone above you—if that role exists—is going to support you in that decision.

Because sometimes, you might not be right.

One of the reasons I was hired by Axon as CFO was to help shift the business more toward subscription services and software. We're so serious about this shift that we decided to put our newest TASER weapon, the TASER 7, on a subscription plan as well. This means that the TASER weapon can effectively be financed for a law enforcement agency. It comes with a number of new analytics within the cloud-based software that provides useful information to the officers and administration.

For the previous iteration of the TASER weapon, we said we had a subscription, but in reality, it was a financing plan. Instead of paying a fee up front, you could stretch your payment out over sixty months. The tech-savvy investors that we wanted to pull into the stock saw right through that and called us on it. I agreed with them and came up with something new for the TASER 7.

I suggested that after the sixty months were up, the agency would have to buy a new weapon, and if they didn't, the weapon would no longer fire. Our CEO, Rick, disagreed. He wanted the new TASER weapon to be such an upgrade with software features so compelling, they'd be clamoring to renew. He didn't want to force anyone into anything.

My pushback was that if the weapon kept functioning after the five-year mark, there was nothing that truly motivated anyone to renew. Officers could just keep using their TASER weapons without the software. In my opinion, if we really wanted to drive a renewal when the subscription ran out, the weapons would have to stop firing.

"If we do that," Rick said, "then there's a chance some officer will pull his gun and shoot someone when he could have used his TASER weapon instead."

That hit me like a proverbial ton of bricks. I couldn't believe my blind spot.

In being the heavy, in trying to effect change in behaviors and outcomes, it is crucial that you don't lose sight of what is the *right* answer. Not just for the company but for people in general. Sometimes, that will mean realizing that what you thought was the right answer actually wasn't. This is the key difference between effective, inspirational leaders and leaders people only listen to because they have to. The former will want to get to the right answer, and the latter is more interested in *being* right.

Be self-aware and recognize when you're wrong. Without hyperbole, you never know when someone's life might depend on it.

BACK TO THE FUTURE

In the next chapter, I'm going to take you back to my journey toward my true North Star, the "guiding light" that determined the choices I made to achieve the goals I had set for myself. Even though I thought I was ready, it turned out I still had a lot of lessons to learn.

So many, in fact, that someone told me I had no business being in the position I was in.

CHAPTER SEVEN

"YOU'RE NOT REMOTELY QUALIFIED TO BE CFO"

It's 2014. At this point, I've had three divisional CFO roles at GE, and during the last one, I went for my MBA at MIT. I entered the program wanting the degree because of experiences at GE that made me realize I wasn't going to learn everything I needed to learn at the company alone. I needed something to augment my education.

DO YOU NEED AN MBA?

A lot of people ask me if they should get their MBA. I struggled with this same question for the first part of my career.

When I started working at GE in the Financial Management Program, my intention was to get a couple of years of leadership development experience and then go get my MBA. However, when I finished those first two years, I had learned so much, and the next program lined up for me (GE's Corporate Audit Staff) was going to only accelerate my development. After I graduated from that program, I had an opportunity to manage a team and work for a senior leader at GE. Then I got a chance to go live abroad as an expat, and after that, it was an opportunity to go learn an entirely new skillset in financial services.

In my first decade at GE, I faced a fork in the road six or seven times where I could either continue the path I was on or leave to go get my MBA. Every time, I looked at the experience I was going to get from the job ahead of me and felt that it would be more valuable to me than an MBA. So I kept pushing the MBA off and thought at one point I may never get it.

Then, during my second CFO role, we spun my business unit out of GE and set up a joint venture with Microsoft to create an entirely new company in the healthcare IT space—Caradigm. I spent a lot of time in Redmond working with Microsoft, as well as with outside lawyers, bankers, and consultants. It was the first time in my career I realized just how much I didn't know and felt like I wasn't going to learn everything I needed to learn as a business leader within the confines of a company like GE. I decided then that I should finally look more seriously at an MBA. At this point, however, I was too far into my career to go back to school full time. I chose an executive MBA program.

In hindsight, I'd do it exactly the same way.

Views are changing on the value of an MBA, but to me it's a no-brainer. Regardless of where you're working, whether in the corporate world or in a small business, you'll absolutely benefit from the frameworks, mental models, and the network you'll build. You can learn a lot about these things online, for free, but there's absolutely no substitute for exchanging ideas with a group of like-minded, similarly driven individuals in a campus setting and in a structured manner led by professional educators.

Why I love the executive or part-time MBA format is you get a lot more out of all of these things.

When you go for your MBA after only a couple of years in the workforce, you don't have enough experience to properly frame up and contextualize what you learn in business school. That's no offense to anyone who's done it—it's simply math. You will get more out of an MBA once you've seen a few business cycles, experienced different economic environments, worked in or with different regions of the world, hired (and fired) some people, managed direct reports, or managed direct reports who have direct reports of their own. These things all generally take more than two or three years to experience. As of this writing, I'm about six years removed from my MBA and often wish I could go back to school with the experiences I've had since then.

What's great about the executive or part-time format is you get a much richer experience not only because you yourself have experienced more, but your classmates have as well. This leads to more valuable discussions in the classroom and in your group assignments, and you also get better interactions with your professors. My class format was Friday and Saturday every other week, which allowed me to try out some of what I learned back at work on Monday. This led to even more engaging conversations back on campus, as my peers and I exchanged notes on our experiences.

So I do recommend that if you're working toward any type of leadership position, you should get your MBA—and the longer you wait to get it, the more you'll get out of it.

Ironically, I started the program with every intention that I was going to stay at GE post-MBA, but toward the end, I had made up my mind that it was time for something new. MIT is a breeding ground not only for entrepreneurs but the entrepreneurial spirit, and I had been bitten by the bug to go be a part of building and growing something at a scale GE couldn't offer. My former admin at GE was now the admin for the CEO of an infrastructure software company, and it turned out they were looking for a new CFO. She mentioned my name to the CEO, and he invited me out for breakfast.

We had a terrific discussion. I had a slide deck that I kept current in terms of my career and the experiences I'd had.

He hadn't seen anything like it from other candidates and was thrilled.

"We would love for you to come on board," he said, "but we're funded by Bain Capital Ventures (BCV), and they have final say in a hire at this level, so you'd have to meet with them next. Can you do that?"

I agreed.

A BIT OF A STRONG FLAVOR

BCV's offices were on one of the top floors of the John Hancock Tower, the tallest building in Boston. For me, having grown up in the suburbs of Boston, going into the city was a big deal. My parents were blue-collar, so to see those skyscrapers as a kid, I thought, *I'll never end up working in one of those buildings.*

And I was about to do a job interview in the Hancock Tower.

Once inside, I met with a few different folks. One happened to be an MIT Sloan alum, and we hit it off right away. It was a good day of interviews. However, the one that mattered the most was with the managing director. He had attended Harvard for undergraduate, then went on to Harvard Business School and had won a number of awards, including being perennially named a Forbes venture capitalist of the year. The man spun gold, and he had the personality to go along with it. The CEO had given me a call before I went in for the interview to give me a heads up.

"Hey, just so you know, he's a bit of a strong flavor," he said, "so don't take anything personally."

Knowing this, I went to the managing director's massive office, the size of two conference rooms put together. His desk was mahogany, and the conference table looked like a varnished section of a sequoia tree with legs. There was a ship's wheel on his wall from the 1800s. His office looked like what a Hollywood studio would conceive for a venture capitalist. He waved me in while he was standing by the window, wrapping up a call, and I sat at his desk, looking at it all in wide-eyed wonder.

The minute he hung up, he sat down across from me and began peppering me with questions. No preamble, no get-to-know-you phase—just right to it. A few minutes in, he stopped.

"Hold on a second," he said. "What job do you think you're interviewing for?"

"For the CFO position," I said.

"Are you kidding me? You're not remotely qualified to be CFO."

Instead of panicking, I decided it was "game on." I saw this as a test.

I was wrong—I just didn't know it yet.

"I disagree that I'm not qualified and here's why." I launched into all the experiences I had at GE and why I believed they prepared me for the role. He pushed back immediately.

"Tell me about a time that you had to help shape the strategy of your business."

I told him about a divestiture I had done at GE, and how we had spun that business off into a joint venture with Microsoft. In fact, it was that experience that made me realize I needed an MBA. Starting a company from scratch, working with bankers and lawyers who were all outside of GE, I realized just how much I didn't know and how much GE couldn't teach me. So I detailed who was involved in that experience and my role in it.

"You're not telling me about strategy," he said. "You're just telling me what happened."

He was right, but I wouldn't admit it. I kept trying to spin it, as well as sharing other stories about times where I had taken a certain action or made some call or shared some insight that drove the strategy. He kept shaking his head.

"Yeah, I'm not getting there," he said. Finally, he stopped me. "Let me ask you a question. Do you think you're ready to be CEO of this company?"

"No, absolutely not."

"There. You see that right there? Do you see that reaction you just had? That's how sure I am that you're not ready to be CFO of this company."

The pummeling continued for another few minutes until I finally realized he wasn't testing me. He legitimately believed I wasn't ready for the position. Enough was enough.

"I realize your time is precious," I told him. "I really appreciate you taking this time with me. I'd like to pivot away from the interview. If you could take whatever meeting time we have left to give me some coaching and guidance as to what I *do* need to do to become a CFO, I would love that."

He took out a piece of paper and began writing down the different paths I could take. I could be a controller somewhere or be the VP of Finance. I needed to get mergers and acquisitions experience and learn how to drive synergies. I needed to have experience with investors and analysts. I needed to be able to articulate a strategy for how to take a company public or how exactly I would raise capital. I needed to be able to demonstrate confidence when it came to relaying the projection and future direction of the business. He walked me through a litany of things that any CFO would need to exhibit.

I wrote everything down, and when it was all done, I thanked him and left. I sent a text to the admin who got this whole thing started.

Well, that was a disaster.

Oh, my God. I'm so sorry. I didn't mean to put you in that position!

No, it's fine.

I was admittedly licking my wounds a bit. Then the CEO, Jack, called.

"So how'd it go?"

"Not good."

"Oh, no, he *loved* you."

"What?

"Yeah, he wants to hire you as VP of Finance, not CFO. He said he thinks that under the right CFO, you'd do terrific. He feels you've got great potential and loved your confidence. He thinks you have a way to go before you're CFO, but he can see it in you."

Needless to say, I wasn't expecting that.

STAY THE COURSE

Not long before this happened, I had given a "fireside chat" to my MBA class at MIT about my career up to that point and about what I was looking to do next. I had articulated all of these things I was looking for:

- I wanted to eventually become a public company CFO, but I wanted to go to a private company for my first standalone CFO job outside of GE. There are only about 3,600 public companies in the United States, so I wanted to learn to walk before I ran (and as you'll soon find out, this was far more important than I had imagined).
- I was looking to work for a tech company, preferably SaaS (software as a service).

- I wanted to be in a company that was well funded. I wanted to play to my strengths as an operator and help a business that was already backed by a few big investors or private equity and not have to worry about raising more capital to keep the company from going under.

Now, here I was being offered a VP of Finance role at a company that checked all these boxes and would have eventually led to a CFO position sometime down the road if I stuck with it.

If I took a number two role, it was a detour. A great number of people did it this way. They take a controller job or a VP role, and then they end up becoming a CFO in their late forties to early fifties. That's fine for those people, but that wasn't the path I had chosen. I told my class and myself that I was going to go straight into another CFO role. Maybe no one would hire me, but I owed it to myself to try. I wanted to grow at an accelerated pace, and I wanted to do it right then and there. I wanted to stay the course toward my North Star.

With all the notes the managing director at BCV had given me, I went back and looked at all the experiences I had at GE and practiced articulating those experiences through the lenses he provided. For example, I hadn't interacted with investors, but I *had* communicated with the leadership at GE corporate, who were essentially investing in my business, and I was accountable to them. As such, I had gone through the motions of knowing my business and understanding how to articulate business performance and strategy. I ensured that I didn't sound like a spectator anymore, that I was actively involved in shaping the strategy and direction of the company.

With that, I dusted myself off and I jumped back in.

Just like that, a recruiter called. I'd been building a relationship with this one for some time, and he let me know that he had an opportunity with another company, Market Track, that checked all the boxes as to what I was looking for.

Armed with my repackaged pitch, I went into that interview with a completely different angle. First, I met with the head of the recruiting firm, as they make you interview with them first. Then it was off to Market Track. I met with the CEO, his executive team, and members of the private equity firm that owned them.

They ended up making me an offer, and I negotiated.

The recruiter called me immediately.

"You have no idea the size of the candidate pool that

applied for this role. You hit the jackpot here. You're going from where you are in your career right now to putting yourself into a different orbit of compensation. Seriously, from here on in, your life is never going to be the same. You sitting here nickel and diming for a few extra dollars of base salary is kind of embarrassing—not just for you but for me. Take what they're giving you."

It was as if you were trying to build a team of baseball players, and one day, you decide to give the janitor a try, and he steps up and throws a ninety-nine-mile-per-hour fastball. When he told me to take the money, he looked at me as if to say yes, you can throw the heat, but you're still the damn janitor.

"Yeah, I appreciate that," I told him, "but this is what I want."

One of the skills that I began cultivating around this time was reading people and trying to understand their motivations. Given how small my ask was, I had a hunch that the recruiter was the one pushing for me to take their offer and that the company probably wouldn't mind. I also thought it important to establish their confidence in me, so I didn't want to just take the first offer on the table. I wanted them to know I understood that a good negotiation outcome really focused on win-win.

So in exchange for a slightly higher salary, I offered to pull forward my start date by two weeks. Even if they turned me down, I really believed the right answer *was* to ask, so I did.

And they gave it to me.

After I started, the CEO later told me that I was always their guy. They had a grid they used to evaluate all the candidates based on specific criteria, and I kept coming out on top on all of the scores. Yes, I was inexperienced compared to the rest of the field, but they couldn't ignore the fact that I always ended up at the top of their list.

One of the biggest factors? The slide deck I had put together articulating why I should be CFO.

I had tailored it to them based on the current challenges they were experiencing and why they had made me the CFO they were seeking. No one else had done that.

I tapped my own shoulder to get the job I truly wanted, and you should too.

LOCATION AGNOSTIC

Be very clear about what you want, and don't compromise on that.

It's easy to get distracted. When I was still at GE, I'd get calls asking me to come be a head of FP&A or a VP of Finance, where they'd increase my compensation by 30 percent. Thirty percent is a meaningful increase, and a lot of people will chase that, particularly if they get to stay in their current company.

Being location agnostic has been incredibly helpful to the growth of my career. I've moved several times. In the thirteen years I was with GE, I moved twelve times. In fact, one of the candidates for my current position at Axon wouldn't move here. I told them that becoming a public company CFO meant I would move anywhere they wanted.

Chase experiences. It can be challenging because it might mean moving away from friends and relationships, but if you're going after what you want, sacrifices will have to be made. The experiences and opportunities I've had have come from those kinds of sacrifices.

This can be especially difficult for those of us from under-represented communities, where a common thread with us, without stereotyping, can be our sometimes disproportionate attachment to our families. I experienced this as a Pakistani American. When I would say how important it was to move away from home, there were many in my community that would say they couldn't leave their parents or extended families. I've seen a number of them miss out on incredible opportunities as a result.

There is no other way I can say this: if you want to make it, you've got to go where the job takes you. Part of tapping your own shoulder means doing what is necessary.

DON'T DEVIATE FROM YOUR NORTH STAR

I'm very open with my team that I want to run a company someday.

That doesn't mean that I'm fielding calls, and I feel like I've already arrived at my North Star in some respects. However, I want to be transparent with them because it's how I got to my seat in the first place.

I also tell them that because I want them to think about their careers in the same way. I want them to follow their North Star and be completely transparent about it in the process.

There is a model for how I think about talent in our organization.

TALENT MODEL

NET TALENT IMPORTER   NET TALENT EXPORTER

◊ Roles you have to go outside to fill   ◊ Talent leaving for outside opportunities

Box 1 represents your company. The talent that you have in the company is represented by the circle contained within the box. If the circle is smaller than your organization or team, then the white space within the box means you need to import talent from elsewhere in the company. These are roles that you have to fill but can't because you don't have the right talent, or you fill them with the wrong talent.

My philosophy is that you should hire in such a way that you have more talent than you need. Yes, you will likely have people who are going to leave because they are ready for the next step but face a lot of competition to get that promotion, but that's a good problem to have. You should build your organization such that you are a net exporter of talent.

It's okay if people leave because that means I have bench strength—it means the person behind them is ready to step up and fill their shoes. If not, I've got to go find someone because the organization isn't overflowing with talent. I want a company full of people whose North Star is trying to be the next CFO or even CEO. Not only does that strengthen the company, but it inspires the individual. They don't feel the need to hide their goals and will do the best job they can, knowing they can be transparent with their ambitions—even if those ambitions take them outside the company.

If one of my direct reports was tapped to be a CFO, or a general counsel, or a CIO somewhere else, I would be thrilled. I would hate to see them go because I love working with all of them, but I'd be happy because they'd be following their own North Star. Taking those jobs would not only mean great things for their careers but for their families as well. I'd be ecstatic to have played some part in that outcome. Not only that, but because I've amassed a group of talented people, it would allow me to continue to promote from within.

IS ANYBODY GOING TO SAY ANYTHING ABOUT THAT ELEPHANT?

Staying the course and following your own North Star go hand in hand—you can't rely on opportunities to present themselves. Eventually, you have to start making them happen for yourself, and part of that might mean moving away from family, even if it goes against what your background might have taught you.

That brings us to the elephant in the room—diversity.

You knew this was coming at some point in this book.

No time to talk about it like the present.

CHAPTER EIGHT

"HOW ARE YOUR VIEWS DIFFERENT FROM ISIS?"

About three months into my new CFO job, the CEO came to talk to me.

"If someone were to ask me how you were doing," he said, "I'd tell them that you're much smarter than we thought, but we knew this learning curve for you was also pretty steep, and it was quite a bit steeper than we thought."

Oh, I thought.

But he was right—it was fair feedback. While I felt like I had gotten my arms around the company and our operations, I was struggling with the accounting organization. The company was growing so fast, doing a number of acquisitions in rapid succession. Some of the basics of "blocking and tackling" just weren't there, and I knew it. I had to step in and do a great deal of it myself. Recruiting was particularly difficult for me because when I was at GE, everyone wanted to work for GE, but no one had heard of this company. It was hard to get good talent to keep up with the growth, and so I ended up doing a lot of it myself.

That would have been okay if I hadn't been learning these processes simultaneously. At GE, there was this immense support network with people there to help and support you. If you didn't answer an email right away or got double-booked for a meeting, it was okay because the machine kept turning. At Market Track, the pace wouldn't allow for it. It hit me in the face like the proverbial fire hose.

In another three months, however, I felt like I finally got my feet underneath me. In October of 2014, we had our first in-person board meeting in New York. The meeting attendees consisted of our senior executive team, members of the private equity firm, and former executives who now served as independent advisors on our board.

The morning of the meeting, one of the board members called me to his hotel room. This was a strange occurrence to me because at GE, visiting people in their hotel rooms was something you didn't do. It just wasn't a good idea. Regardless, it was a board member, so I went.

When I arrived, he said, "Let's have breakfast."

There was a sitting area at the far end of his room where all the food was laid out that he'd had delivered to the room. Sipping his coffee, he started the conversation talking about the state of the world and how crazy things are in the Middle East and the general turmoil there.

Exactly. You're thinking what I was thinking: *Where is he going with this?*

He started narrowing in a bit by talking specifically about what was happening in Iraq and with ISIS.

"I've done a lot of reading. I tend to read a lot, and I like to get other people's perspectives," he said. He was shucking and jiving. I could tell he was trying to very delicately get to his point—except when he did, there was nothing delicate about it.

Finally, he said, "Look, I've read about ISIS and their philosophy, and what strikes me as interesting is that these guys believe that they are interpreting their religion in the Qur'an literally. They're not extremists. People tend to paint them as extremists, but from what I've read, they're not. They truly believe they're following their religion. So I was very curious to know your thoughts on that because you profess to be Muslim as well, so what I'm asking is: How are your beliefs different from ISIS?"

I was floored—and temporarily speechless.

"Well, I'm not very religious. I'm spiritual. I try to follow the tenets of the religion, and while it is my faith, I try to find a balance. I try to live a good life and be a good person, and I don't think that what they're doing in terms of the violence and beheadings in any way represents what's in the Qur'an. I don't support that at all. I *do* feel that it's an extreme interpretation."

I went on to explain how the Qur'an was designed to be purposefully vague in order to let people think and reach their own conclusions—that Islam is not the type of religion where things are prescriptive. The problem with that is then you have sects of people who interpret it very strictly. For example, nowhere in the Qur'an does it say that women need to be covered from head to toe. *Nowhere.* My wife is a practicing Muslim and *is* very religious, and she does *not* wear a burqa.

When I said this, it seemed as though I was giving him what he was looking for. My feeling is that the reason he brought it up in the first place was that this meeting was going to be the first time everyone was face-to-face with their new CFO, and he wanted to be sure I wasn't going to make some offhand comment about the infidels later at dinner.

It's crazy, I know, but it's the only explanation I have for why he chose *that* moment to have *that* conversation, and make no mistake, I'm not excusing it. It's the only thing that makes sense. I had met with him several times before, and this had never come up.

The board meeting ended up going quite well, and we debriefed later in the hallway. We agreed on next steps to take business-wise, and as he walked away, he turned around and said, "Hey, good job," and gave me two thumbs up. It actually made me feel good in the moment because he had given me some rough feedback as related to the difficulties I'd been having. The odd and somewhat inappropriate conversation seemed to have moved to the rearview. I'd hoped it was an isolated incident and that it would be the last time I'd encounter something like that during my time there.

What is that saying about hoping in one hand and shitting in the other?

YOU CALLED HER A *WHAT?*

At Market Track, I not only owned finance, but I was also in charge of HR and the legal departments. While that seemed like a lot of work, I was actually excited about it when I took the job because at GE, I was very big on people development. It was one of my favorite aspects of the job.

What I didn't realize is that part of what comes with HR is all the benefits paperwork as well as dealing with employee complaints. GE was the type of company where they were very clear about integrity. It was a world-class organization with world-class talent, and it was an exceedingly odd thing for someone to make an off-color joke in a meeting or anything of that nature. You could get fired for that, plain and simple.

Market Track was not like GE.

Market Track was much smaller, and a number of employees had recently come from other businesses or through an acquisition. Another executive had previously worked at another company where he brought almost his entire team over. It was very much a bro culture. Many of them had gone to college together, and they all played sports. It was macho, jockish, and not at all inclusive.

This group made off-color comments constantly, to the

point where we were in a meeting in that executive's office, and a woman walked by, and he stopped me from talking to say, "Dude, check that out."

"Can we focus?" I said. "I'm trying to have a conversation with you." He then proceeded to call in one of his team and ask inappropriate questions about the woman in question, with all kinds of innuendos, sending them into fits of snickering.

Our CEO lived in another city and wasn't around enough to witness the behavior, which only made matters worse. It was an incredibly toxic culture, so I was fielding complaints about these kinds of things all the time.

There was a woman, Robin, who was managing a small team. She was extremely competent and very assertive. One night, one of her male direct reports was out with another one of her female team members. They were at a bar and started making fun of Robin, talking about what a hard-ass she was. In the midst of this, they took a selfie together and posted it on Instagram, with the title "Robin is a cunt."

Robin followed one of them on Instagram, so of course she saw this. She took a screenshot and brought it to me in tears. I apologized that she was going through this and told her I would take care of it.

We had a call with the CEO along with the rest of the leadership for that division, and I said, without reservation, that the male reporting to Robin needed to be fired. Robin was beyond upset and was rightfully quite concerned about facing this guy when he came back to work.

In my opinion, there are words in the English language that are simply unutterable. That is absolutely one of them. While this could have been a learning experience for him, he was going to have to take that lesson with him somewhere else.

The reaction was predictable and disappointing.

"Hold on a second," they said. "You might be overreacting here. He's a young guy, and he made a mistake. We shouldn't penalize him for it."

I was beside myself with anger. "What are you guys talking about? Are you proposing we just slap him on the wrist, and he comes back to work so Robin has to see him every day? How would you guys feel if it was someone you knew? A family member?"

"Look, this is a delicate situation," the CEO said. He decided to involve an outside attorney, an older woman very deep into her career. We had used her services for other situations in the past, so the CEO leaned on her again.

We had a call with her, and I laid out all the facts.

Her reaction was unpredictable and disappointing.

"This is an unfortunate situation, but I suggest a reprimand and a month's suspension."

"Excuse me," I said, "but I don't agree with that. I think this is a fireable offense."

"And I think you're overreacting. I've been called that word so many times over my career I've lost count."

I was stunned. "I'm sorry that happened to you, but that's irrelevant here. In this day and age, this is not okay."

Then she came with the left hook. "You know what's interesting to me? It seems like you've got some sort of agenda here. It seems strange to me that you're pushing so hard for this man to be fired."

"That's absurd to the point of being insulting," I said.

"Look how upset you're getting. You've proven my point. This is clearly an emotional topic for you. You're not qualified to make this call, given your feelings about the situation."

That was the nail in the coffin. There was overwhelming

opposition to my wanting to remove this individual, so my hands were essentially tied. As a result, the employee was suspended for six weeks without pay. Robin had to work with him again, and though he apologized, I could see that she was uncomfortable.

That took me beyond the boiling point, and after a number of more minor incidents came up to my level, I decided that Market Track was going to have sensitivity training.

I worked with another lawyer on labor law and other employment issues. He was based out of Chicago and really terrific. He was very forward-thinking and always gave me solid, actionable advice. He came out to see the status of our company and then put together a slide deck presentation for me.

As you can imagine, it wasn't good.

"Jawad, I have never seen another company with as many issues as yours. You guys are sitting on a ticking time bomb. It's really only a matter of time before you guys get sued."

CULTURE ISN'T JUST CHECKING BOXES

We went through the training, which, unsurprisingly, didn't make all that much of a difference. As time went on, our CEO moved into an executive chair role. The new

CEO was based in Chicago, near our HQ, and came from a big organization that focused on inclusivity. He recognized immediately that we had a huge culture problem.

He decided he wanted to appoint a female head of that problematic division.

There was an outside woman who was the runner-up for the CEO position. When she didn't get it, she wrote to thank us for the opportunity and told us how much she loved the company and hoped to be a part of it. The new CEO offered her the division head role, thinking this would be the first step in helping to change the culture.

It does no good, however, to cut the head off a snake if there are still a bunch more in the nest. All of the "dude bros" that she had inherited who had remained in the organization made her life incredibly difficult.

Sadly, I found out after I left that she didn't last long in the role, but I was there long enough to see that it likely stemmed from a team that was attempting to undercut her at every turn with their toxicity.

Market Track was sold after I left, and the new private equity firm that took over made everyone reapply for their jobs. They were run through intelligence and personality tests. I was told later that the majority of the toxic jocks didn't make it through, and the ones that did were managed out quickly thereafter.

Through all of this, we learned that we had attempted to fix the problem by effectively checking a diversity box when the problem was that our culture was rotten to the core. You can't make the decision to hire someone from a marginalized community and expect them to fix the problems that already exist.

You have a responsibility as a leader to shape not only your direct team, but your leadership peers. You cannot be complicit. It was the reason I led the call for a new head of that division. I viewed it as my responsibility not only to the organization but to create an imprint on the company as a whole. I saw firsthand the people suffering and struggling due to the toxicity of our culture, and to stand by and do nothing about it meant I was effectively endorsing it.

SHORT-TERM VERSUS LONG-TERM DECISIONS

I'd like to tell you that my story with Market Track at the beginning of this chapter was over, but before we tackled the issue of our toxic culture, I had more lessons to learn about how to be the leader I wanted to become. It was all about playing the long game, and not getting shortsighted.

And I'll tell you all about it in the next chapter.

CHAPTER NINE

"WHO TOLD YOU TO DO THAT?"

Back to my CEO at my first standalone CFO job.

I mentioned in the previous chapter that things got off to a rocky start, particularly on the accounting side of things. Moving into the fourth quarter of my first year, I was still struggling with those issues and essentially trying to brute force my way into keeping everything together.

Then I got a call from our assistant controller who was in Upstate New York. I had essentially inherited a team of accountants in Saratoga Springs, which was not exactly a hotbed of financial talent by any stretch of the imagination. The controller had been trying to get in touch with me, but I was in the midst of so much chaos that we had difficulty connecting. I asked him via email if there was anything urgent I needed to know, and he told me it could wait until the following week.

Turns out it couldn't.

We finally connected by phone and he asked me, "What are we going to do about payroll next week?"

"What do you mean?" I said.

"Well, we don't have enough cash to cover payroll next week."

The sinking feeling was almost enough to pull me out of my chair. "What do you mean we don't have enough?"

"Well, our sales team has been adding contracts without identifying a billing contact at the customer, so we haven't been tracking very well on our accounts receivable. Those customers we have billed haven't been paying us on time. Also, I don't need to remind you that we've been on an acquisition spree, and our payroll keeps getting bigger by the month. We just don't have enough cash."

I was done. So many thoughts were racing through my mind. First, this was exactly the kind of thing my CEO had been worried about. I also pictured that interview I had with Bain Capital Ventures and how I was told to go learn the ropes first before making the leap to CFO. And I kept wracking my brain as to how my time at GE didn't prepare me for this when it prepared me so well for most other aspects of the job.

As a divisional CFO, you didn't have to worry about cash, or anything on the balance sheet really, because GE Treasury swept the cash from its business units and managed it centrally. Not having enough cash to make payroll was therefore something I had never considered as a possibility from my time at GE, but I kept reminding myself that this is exactly the kind of reason why I left GE—so I would have had the chance to learn how to deal with a crisis like this.

None of that mattered now. I needed to figure it out. So I sprang into action. We started calling customers and imploring them to make sure they paid their bills on time to get some cash in the door. We pushed off whatever expenses we could. We stopped paying vendors on time to push things out even further, and that still wasn't enough. I had to fall back on our revolver.

A revolver is essentially a credit facility that you can draw on at any time. We had one of about $10 million, and we had never pulled from it until this moment. We took a loan against it and made payroll. Pushing the customers to pay and extending payments to vendors is part of managing your working capital and nothing all that newsworthy. Drawing from a revolver means you're taking on additional debt and is the kind of thing you need to let your CEO and board know about.

Needless to say, they were less than enthused when I called them.

"Our cash situation is tight. I'm working on updating our cash forecasts, but we're still having trouble with our receivables, and our payroll is burgeoning with all of these companies that we've acquired. I'm doing the best I can with the pieces I have."

And that was true. I had not gone out and hired specific roles to help support our growth, with the exception of a controller I hired on at probably half of what I should have paid, all in order to stay within a budget. It was the mindset I had brought with me from GE—you never missed your numbers. The finance team was woefully understaffed, but with the overwhelming focus on profitability, I didn't feel that I could spend to add talent. The problem was that in taking this approach, I skimped my way into a mediocre accounting team, and they delivered exactly what I had paid for.

We got to January when we closed the books for the entire year, and it came time to talk about my performance review.

"So this first year has been a bit of a struggle for you," he said.

Not a great way to begin a review. It got worse. Part of my annual bonus was tied to company goals, and the other half was discretionary—namely my CEO's discretion.

"I'm going to cut your bonus in half," he told me.

When you get paid 50 percent of your bonus, you're being sent a very clear message.

"That is a huge chunk of my income," I said. "This is unacceptable."

"We hired you to figure out all the issues we had, and you're not doing it."

"I've been trying, but there are so many other factors that were in play before I ever started here. The accounting in this organization has been neglected for so long. I was trying to get up to speed in a way that saved the business money because I knew that it was important to you to show the private equity company that we're hitting our profit numbers. I built this team for pennies on the dollar to hit those numbers."

"Well, who told you to do that?"

The question took me aback. I thought, *Shit, he's right. No one actually told me I needed to do that.*

SHORT-TERM PAIN FOR LONG-TERM GAIN

I realized that I was operating under assumptions that were untrue, or at the very least, irrelevant. At GE, you had to stick to your budget, and if you came in under at the end of the year, you were celebrated. That had been ingrained into my mindset.

One of the reasons I didn't upgrade the team was budgetary. The other was because I didn't want to turn over the team because, as mediocre as they were, they were doing a job. I was worried that if I started to turn over one or two of them, then I was going to have a mass exodus on my hands, and they were all going to quit.

The truth was that my team was in way over their heads. I needed people to support me and should have brought those people in. If the team ended up quitting, fine. They quit, and I could have brought in consultants.

Even if it meant suffering a short-term pain, in the long term, we would have been so much better off.

This is a big issue I see today with my own direct reports when they have low performers they don't want to turn over. They're only thinking about the short-term and all of the extra work that will fall onto their plate, or they worry about something big getting missed as a result. They're not wrong that there is some risk of that, but they'll suffer in the long-term if they don't take that risk.

Employees that are mediocre don't often have the self-awareness to know that they are, and they will rarely remove themselves from their situation or look to improve. The other employees on the team who are carrying their weight will absolutely notice, and it's demotivating to see a substandard team member continue to stick around. It sounds harsh, but as a leader, if your team is going to trust and follow you, you have to make better decisions than leaving warm bodies in the chair. Their low performance will only cause the team to suffer.

Suffer the short-term pain for the long-term success of the team.

OVER BUDGET AND IN CONTROL

I brought the lesson from Market Track to Axon.

When I arrived at Axon, I once again inherited a team comprising mostly accountants—we didn't have any-where near the type of finance organization that a public company should have. There are a lot more reporting requirements when you're public, and it costs an additional $2 million to $3 million in expenses because there are roles and capabilities that need to be filled that don't exist when you're a private company. Axon had been public for a while when I had joined but hadn't made the necessary investments in its finance function.

I wasn't going to repeat my previous mistake. I was going to spend whatever it took to get the team I wanted.

The best part? When I was taking the job, I was clear about what I intended to do to upgrade our finance team. Our CEO said, "Jawad, go do what you need to do. We're going to support you. Build your team, and don't worry about going over budget."

It was such a different experience and a welcoming feeling. When you go over budget to build your team, that's a pain you experience exactly once. If you avoid that pain and skimp on the money it takes to bring in the absolute best talent, the long-term pain is unavoidable and immeasurable because day to day, month to month, and quarter to quarter, chances are your people are missing key things that will end up losing you far more money than if you had gone ahead and spent it on better talent.

In bringing this philosophy to Axon, the position of CFO took on a new meaning. Once I put my management team in place, we went to work hiring the right people and leveling up the compensation. Finance was not seen as a priority previously. People saw the CFO as someone who oversaw closing the books.

So I set to work to change that perception. I clearly defined the pillars of my new finance organization—accounting, financial planning and analysis (FP&A), investor relations (IR), and corporate strategy.

Job number one was fixing the accounting organization, which involved hiring a new controller and leveling up the talent. We not only focused on improving the integrity of our financial statements; we set out to establish processes and controls that would help drive improved rigor across the entire organization.

We shifted the focus of the FP&A team from weather reporting to being true business partners who worked with the operational leaders in the business to set budgets and establish long-range forecasts.

There was no in-house IR at the time, so I set out to recruit a transformational leader for that role who would help shift the perception of the business from weapons manufacturer to cutting-edge tech/SaaS company. I worked with one of our board members from a corporate strategy standpoint to define a capital allocation strategy.

In short, I pushed hard (and spent) to build a finance function that would be seen as a thought leader that set the tone and pace for our internal functions. I couldn't have done it without the support of Rick, our CEO, the other executives, our board, and most importantly, the team I put in place to execute on that vision.

People see that vision now, and it's awesome. As a result of the work we've done here, they've tasked me with doing the same in the IT and legal departments. There was no trick to it—the strategy was the same.

Hire the best people, no matter what it costs.

DON'T TRIP ON YOUR VICTORY LAP

I'll be the first to admit that some of this sounds a bit self-aggrandizing, that my arm might be a little tired and overstretched from patting myself on the back. Sometimes being confident and proud of what you accomplished can cross into that territory, and it's something you have to be cognizant of.

Ask me how I know.

CHAPTER TEN

———

"DON'T DRAPE YOURSELF IN ROSES"

While I'd had a rough early start in my first standalone CFO position, I found my footing and got comfortable in the role. We started firing on all cylinders, doing more acquisitions, and the company began to grow quite quickly.

Private equity firms have tried-and-true structures. Large institutional investors, such as pension funds and other accredited investors, put their capital to work with private equity firms, who make the calls as to where to invest. They make very calculated decisions about how to deploy the capital, and the main strategy is to take an ownership stake in a privately held company that can become a plat-form from which they can grow both organically and by bolting on acquisitions. We were one such platform. We had a web-based software for helping companies figure out how effective their marketing and advertising spend was.

They then bolted on other companies that did something similar to what we did with the goal of getting it large enough to sell. It's almost like flipping a house. You buy a house as your platform using money you mostly borrowed. You put in a new kitchen and a pool and finish the attic to flip it for a profit. Whoever loaned you the money gets some return on their investment, and you keep the rest. That's essentially how private equity works.

As with most things in life, explaining something simply is easy to do, but actually executing on it is much more difficult. These private equity firms are incredibly talented at raising money, identifying great companies to buy, and then selling these companies for a profit. However, for the most part, they do not have expertise in actually running the companies they've purchased because, well, that's not what they do. They are investors, not operators.

Back to our house analogy.

When you put a new kitchen in a house that you're trying to flip, there's nothing left for you to do once you finish it. But companies are collections of people, teeming with their own culture, politics, systems, and processes, and they are notoriously difficult to integrate with another company. So simply buying a business, bolting it on to your existing investment, and hoping for the best is not a winning strategy. You need operators to do the hard work of integrating these acquisitions while they are also running their day-to-day business.

The management teams at the companies are expected to take care of those operations. When, however, you have a portfolio of companies and a sizeable amount of assets under management (we're talking in the billions), you can attract some outstanding folks who have distinguished themselves as world-class operators.

For this reason, private equity firms bring on advisors and a board of directors for each company, as well as an executive advisory board that sits over the entire portfolio of companies. This advisory board usually recruits people who acquired an extremely useful amount of operational, day-to-day skills and knowledge in the corporate world, which they've since left. They're hired to attend a few meetings throughout the year, or more commonly, members of the portfolio companies come to meet with them to pitch their strategic outlook or report on budgets for the previous and coming years.

During my time there, Larry Bossidy served on this advisory board. Larry was a longtime executive at GE and the former CEO and chairman of AlliedSignal (later Honeywell) in the 1990s. Incidentally, Larry started his career at GE in the same financial leadership development program that I did, a point he liked to reminisce about the two to three times a year that I saw him.

Although Larry left GE long before I started there, he was a legend at the company. One of the hallmarks of GE management was strong execution, and Larry wrote the book on execution—literally. His book *Execution: The Discipline of Getting Things Done,* with Ram Charan, is one of the best on this topic.

I mentioned earlier that I don't get starstruck. In one of the great ironies in life, I tend to run into celebrities on a fairly regular basis. I've had a chance to meet probably four to five dozen celebrities in my life, and the only time I ever asked for an autograph was when President George H. W. Bush visited Raytheon, where my mother worked, when I was in fourth grade. I've encountered famous actors or athletes in various social settings, at corporate events, fundraisers, or sat next to them on flights. Every time it happens, all I can think of is how much I would value my own privacy if I were in their shoes, so I keep to myself. I also happen to measure my life in terms of how much I accomplish, not who I meet.

That said, the first time I met Larry, I was starstruck.

The private equity firm that owned Market Track would get all of its portfolio companies together twice a year: once in April to pitch a long-term strategic outlook and once in December to review the year's results and the upcoming year's budgets.

The way these meetings were run, the private equity firm would have all thirty or so of its employees on hand to listen to the presentations. There were another ten or so members of this executive advisory board in the room. They would then call each of the management teams—typically only the CEO, CFO, and one or two other execs—from the portfolio companies into the room one by one to give their presentation.

The first time I met Larry was in April of 2014, a few weeks after I started on the job. He was more or less eighty years old at the time, and the first thing that struck me was how he absolutely commanded the room. He had a booming voice and intense gaze, and despite his advanced age, you could tell that there was still a bright fire burning behind his eyes. But he was also disarming. He had a sharp wit and sense of humor that made you want to get on his radar so you could share in that energy.

In my first meeting with Larry, I was too new to contribute anything, but he made me feel welcome by telling everyone in the room that we had a common background at GE.

Larry had worked on the Corporate Audit Staff after he did the Financial Management Program—as I had done—and while he was welcoming, he clearly set the tone that he expected great things from me.

At our meeting in December of that year, I was in the midst of my early struggles and didn't have a ton to celebrate. The business had an okay year, but it wasn't anything to write home about. I promised myself that by the following year, I'd have something for Larry to gush over.

At our December 2015 meeting, we had great things to report. We had ended up having a terrific year. I finally felt like I had gotten my feet under me and was helping drive great business results.

This particular meeting was in Los Angeles, at the private equity firm's headquarters. They were in a high-rise in Westwood, and from the lobby, you could see a spectacular view of Santa Monica and the Pacific Ocean. Our CEO, myself, and a couple of other members of our executive team were waiting to be called into the conference room, and we were in a good mood as we rehearsed our talking points.

We went in there in heavy victory-lap mode talking about all the things we had accomplished. We exceeded our revenue growth, bookings, and profitability targets. All the other key indicators were running smooth as silk. I told them how good they should have been feeling about their investment in us before diving deeper into the highlights of our financials.

Larry sat and listened to my spiel. We were sitting at the conference room table across from one another, and at one point, he held his hand up. The room fell silent, and everyone leaned in to hear what he was going to say next.

"You had a good year," he said, "but don't go draping yourself in roses just yet."

He started pointing out weak spots in the financials. Our SG&A (sales, general, and administrative expenses) as a percentage of revenue was 25 percent when it should have been 20 percent. We had add-backs where we essentially treated certain expenses as one-time items that were excluded from our operating margin, thereby boosting our profits. Larry pointed out that most companies would treat these as recurring expenses and not adjust them out. For example, when someone from an acquisition was fired and paid severance, we shouldn't have treated it like it didn't happen—things like that happen on an ongoing basis.

Even though the discussion maintained a positive tone, once again, I found myself thinking, *Shit, he's right.*

STAY GROUNDED

Right or wrong, people will always find things to criticize. It *is* important to project confidence, without a doubt—to be optimistic and upbeat for our employees, our investors, or whoever your audience might be. Do so, however, without draping yourself in roses. Temper your exuberance a bit. You can remain confident, upbeat, and positive, but you must be mindful of how you come across.

You must be self-critical. You can't be so optimistic that you leave yourself open to further criticism.

At Axon, when we prepare for our earnings calls, we have a script that the CEO, the president, and I read about our results. Once we've finished with the transcript, we open up the call to questions, and you have no idea what kinds of questions are coming. As such, a lot of what we do is try to anticipate and prepare for what they might be.

Because of that experience at Market Track, part of my preparation includes me not just being self-congratulatory about all of our successes—I also anticipate where people could poke holes in the reporting of our success. That advice from Larry has been immensely helpful to me as a public company CFO because it is a constant reminder for me to step back and be more self-critical than I've ever been. It prepares me for the tough questions that might come.

WRITE YOUR OWN TICKET—CAREFULLY

When Rick, the CEO of Axon first made me an offer, he told me to write my own ticket.

"What does that mean?" I asked him.

"I'm going to give you a piece of paper, and want you to write down what you want for your compensation."

I was taken aback. It was the stuff you see in the movies. You don't think this happens in real life. Considering my past experience, I thought this was a test. Not wanting to drape myself in roses, I didn't want to put down some enormous number without having proven myself. I also didn't want to insult him and the board. I went to the Axon president, Luke, and asked him for some advice.

"Well, the previous CFO's compensation was public. Go look it up. Then, based on whatever you think you bring to the table, you can tweak it from there."

I thought on it for a bit, but not for long.

Soon after, I came back to Rick asking for slightly *less* than what the previous CFO had made. He had been there for thirteen years and had built a solid relationship with the team. I decided that I wasn't going to negotiate this time—I was going to demonstrate my worth.

LET YOUR WORK SPEAK FOR ITSELF

By the time you read this book, Axon will have released its annual proxy with all of the compensation details for the public officers in the company. It will have the details of the new nine-year plan that Rick, our CEO, placed us all on. In short, I went from taking a decreased compensation package to being locked up through 2030. I will essentially be able to retire from Axon with a team I helped build and a business that has a vital and critical mission.

Had I come in asking for more money without proving myself, I could be telling you an entirely different story right now. But because I learned not to drape myself in roses and let my work speak for itself, I'm finding myself in a position I never could have imagined.

Once I got in the door, based on what I had learned about getting what you paid for, it was time to upgrade the finance team—the right way.

And I knew just where to start.

CHAPTER ELEVEN

"I KNOW WHY YOU'RE CALLING, AND THE ANSWER IS NO"

In 2017, after leaving behind the toxicity of Market Track, I finally landed in my home—Axon.

When I was at Market Track, prior to my epiphany about spending the money to get the right people in place, I had tried to recruit someone for the controller position that I had worked with in the past who had also become a friend: Jim.

In terms of risk-taking, Jim was one of the most conservative guys I'd ever met—very risk-averse. Everything he does is done with meticulous consideration, listing out all the possible pros and cons. He thinks of all the ways something can go wrong, and even if he can't identify all of them, he wants to have taken that line of thought to its logical end so he can determine whether or not said endeavor is a risk worth taking.

It was because of this trait that he turned me down. He'd ask me questions such as:

- "What if I move my family out there and it doesn't work out?"
- "What if you leave?"
- "What if the company goes under?"

Granted, it was frustrating from a recruiting standpoint, but it was these qualities that made him an excellent controller. He did the kind of work that helped you sleep better at night because you knew he was considering every possible angle in every possible situation.

Which is exactly why I had to have him at Axon.

Once I'd settled in, I got on the phone. A press release had gone out about my hiring, and it was all over my LinkedIn, so I knew there was a better than average chance that he knew I'd landed the position. When he picked up the phone, he didn't even say hello.

"I know why you're calling," he said, "and the answer is no."

"Jim, just hear me out, man."

"I will, but I'm betting this pitch won't be much different from the one you gave me at the last company. I've already been through the thought process about whether or not I wanted to leave GE, and we know how that turned out."

NOT JUST COMPENSATION

He was right, but when I had tried to recruit him previously, I was still in the GE mentality myself. I thought I had to stay on budget to get him.

Not this time. Even better, from that situation, I came to the understanding that not skimping wasn't just about bumping up the compensation package.

"I want to fly you *and* your family out here to Arizona," I told him.

We didn't just put them on a plane—they all got first-class tickets. When they landed, we had them taken to the Fairmont, which is a beautiful resort in Scottsdale. The red carpet had been rolled out.

Before he arrived to meet with me and the CEO, I asked

all of the executives to put on the full-court press. Rick told him all about his mission to change the world by making the bullet obsolete. Rick is a force of nature—he invented the TASER weapon and turned it into a ubiquitous product that is now a household name, and then he went and did it again with body cameras, and he's going to do it yet again with software. That is to say, he makes it easy to get behind him and buy into his mission. This was the first thing we had going for us in getting Jim to make the jump.

The second was that where Market Track was privately owned, Axon is a public company. That's a big feather in the cap for anyone who's working in finance. Being a controller of a public company is no small feat.

He also had the benefit of coming into a familiar environment in the sense that we had worked together before—he was my controller at GE. He knew I wasn't a micromanager and as such, he had the ability to say no to me. In fact, Jim tells me no more than my kids do. He always tells me when I'm wrong. He has no fear of me, and he doesn't look at me in some starry-eyed fashion. He tells it like it is and keeps me honest.

On top of all that, Jim has his CPA, something I don't have. In a lot of respects, he's a better pure finance person than I am.

All this to say, I wanted Jim at Axon. I *needed* Jim at Axon. And I was going to get Jim at Axon.

INTEGRITY

Jim is a beacon of integrity. In addition to being risk-averse, he's a structured thinker, and it's what makes him a great controller. It's also what helps me—and I'd imagine the rest of the team—sleep at night. He considers everything that might go wrong and sees around every corner.

Because he does this so well, there are times when I want to make certain calls, especially ones pertaining to accounting or compensation-related issues, and Jim will hold the line based on his interpretation of accounting guidance. He is very clear-eyed and objective about looking at the optics of a situation as well as doing the right thing. He's always putting himself in the shoes of both the employees and the shareholders, and he has no issue standing up to senior leadership and telling them that they're wrong.

Jim has a steel backbone. It holds true not just in his work but in his personal life as well. I'm proud to work with him as well as call him a friend.

If he agreed to come, he was getting the keys to the bus. By that, I meant I would essentially hand him the accounting team, and that's exactly what I did. That group of thirty to forty people had seen me as their leader, but I wanted them to see Jim in that light. I physically moved them into a different space in a different building so they would all be together, and I moved Jim's desk right there with them.

Now Jim is doing exactly what he dreamed he'd be doing, and he's having a blast. While he has no current aspiration to be a CFO, he knows he's now in a culture where he can have that goal and not have to keep it a secret. He's managing a large team already, and they love him.

Those material weaknesses I mentioned earlier in the book? Jim put a rock-star team in place that resolved them, and the auditors love him for that. He's been a fantastic hire.

And I wouldn't have been able to do that had I not realized that you must relentlessly pursue top talent.

IT DOES COST, BUT IT ALSO PAYS

None of this came cheap, however.

In order to get Jim here, we gave him a rich base salary and a big bonus. We also gave him a mix of restricted stock units (RSUs) and performance restricted stock units (PRSUs). RSUs are time-based, which means they vest at annual milestones. PRSUs are tied to actual performance goals.

We essentially told him that he had a certain time frame

in which to remediate not only the existing material weaknesses but also any new ones that might pop up after he started. Prior to his arrival, we were relying on contractors for a large portion of our accounting work, spending over $3 million a year (and doing a very poor job to boot). He had to cut that spending by a third and bring all of those outsourced functions in-house, such as tax, internal audit, and revenue accounting. I told him that if he was able to hit these goals by a certain time, it would be the demonstration of a healthy accounting organization, and as such, if he hit a certain number of those goals, he'd get 100 percent of his stock award, and if he hit all the goals, he'd get 200 percent. Twice the stock—not an insignificant amount.

I don't tell you this to brag about what we were able to do for him or to air his finances publicly. If you're a leader who is still mired in the idea of going on the cheap when it comes to recruiting, I want you to use the above as an example of what you can and should do when it comes to bringing the absolute best talent to your organization.

You should do it because it pays dividends.

Doing all those things to make sure that Jim—as well as the other great talent we've hired on his team since then—was as financially set as we could possibly make him has added, without hyperbole, hundreds of millions of dollars to our market cap.

Yes, you read that correctly. The amount of value that Jim created for the company has been incredible. We can trust our financials, which means investors can buy the stock without worrying about the integrity of them.

Jim isn't the only rock star I was able to bring aboard with this new philosophy in hand.

Remember AJ from previous chapters? Luke, Axon's president, put me in touch with AJ because we recognized that we needed to up our game in the investor relations department. The previous CFO had been handling it all himself, and we knew that we needed someone to handle this important task full time, not just as a part-time hobby.

AJ was the number two in investor relations at Tesla before the head of the department quit. She was doing such a good job filling in that she had an opportunity to be the head. On Luke's recommendation, I contacted her immediately. He didn't think that I would be able to pull her away from Tesla but that she might have some potential candidates in mind.

"Here's what I'm looking to do," I told her. "I need someone with a lot of energy and an outsized personality, someone investors are really going to identify with in this fast-growing tech company." There was an image of us as a fast-growing tech organization that I wanted to project because that's who Axon is. Two days after I joined, we changed the name from TASER to Axon, and it was a big part of why I joined, because we were transforming into something more, and I wanted our investor relations messaging to reflect that.

AJ gave me a list of about eight different names of people who fit the profile. I spent a lot of time researching them, and no one was doing it for me. Two hours later, when I had gotten to the bottom of the list, I felt completely underwhelmed. I sat back in my chair, arms folded, and thought. I didn't know anyone I could pull from my GE days. Most of the investor relations folks I knew there were pretty senior and wouldn't come work for me.

On a whim, I sat forward at my keyboard and started researching AJ. All of this exciting information popped up. She had started her career as a journalist. From there she went to work for Dougherty & Company, a boutique investment firm, and while working for them, she was the analyst covering TASER.

What really stood out was what happened when she was also covering Tesla. After having success with their Model S, they announced they were releasing an SUV, the Model

X. However, they were having issues scaling, and most analysts had the stock price targeted at a hundred dollars. Then they had some additional stumbles, and the majority dropped their price target to fifty dollars.

AJ raised hers from $100 to $300 and publicly stated why everyone had it wrong and why they would succeed. This put her all over the news, from CNN to Bloomberg Financial to CNBC. You can still see the videos on YouTube today, and they are worth searching if for no other reason than the sheer entertainment value of seeing all of these so-called experts mansplaining to AJ what she apparently got wrong about Tesla and electric cars. Everyone wanted to know what this woman—in a male-dominated field— saw that no one else was seeing. In the footage, she was passionate and confident about her stance and for good reason.

She was right. The Model X was a smash success. Their stock price has since gone soaring over $300. Everything she said came to fruition. It was no wonder Tesla had hired her.

All this to say, I wanted AJ at Axon. I *needed* AJ at Axon. And I was going to *get* AJ at Axon.

I asked her for another call to thank her for sending over the list.

"I went through the names in a lot of detail," I said, "but the person I felt the best about wasn't on the list. It was you."

She laughed. "I'm very flattered, thank you very much, but I'm really happy at Tesla."

"Hear me out," I said. "I know you're familiar with the company and we've changed a lot since you followed us as an analyst. We're not just TASER anymore. We're Axon. We're trying to save lives, not just with the TASER weapon, but also by building a fairer justice system and trying to bring more transparency to police."

It resonated with her. She was also living in Seattle and would have to move to take the position at Tesla, something she was not excited to do. We had a big software office in Seattle, and I told her we would let her work from there. Even though our headquarters is in Scottsdale, I didn't care where she worked as long as the work got done. That opened the door to talk about my management style, and I put her in touch with my direct reports. She then spoke with Luke and Rick, which only helped to sweeten the idea.

"I'm actually pretty interested," she said, "but I really love Tesla and our mission."

You know what came next.

MAKE PEOPLE FEEL WANTED

"I'd love to bring you and your family to Scottsdale. Let me roll out the red carpet for you the way Axon did for me."

"You don't need to do that."

But I did. And as a leader, you do too.

It feels good to be wanted. To be wined and dined. Everyone should get to experience that.

We flew her family down first class and put them up at a resort with a lazy river, which I hoped her kids would enjoy. I took my family out there and had dinner with them.

While there, she said, "No one's ever done anything like this for me."

I'll admit, that made me somewhat sad to hear because I knew it was true. In all of my work experience, I'd always seen companies go the extra mile to attract talent, but typically only for executives and typically only for the men. When it came to recruiting executive women, I didn't see *any* of this. The attitude seemed to me to be that because they were women, they were fortunate just to be getting the opportunity.

Obviously, AJ accepted, and just like Jim, she has added

hundreds of millions of dollars of value to the organization. She has been so incredibly effective and not just at her job in investor relations. She's a great student of business and understands how all the pieces fit together. She helps me with corporate strategy, so we promoted her. Her role today is vice president of Corporate Strategy and Investor Relations.

LOYALTY LEADS TO RESILIENCY

One of the reasons my team is so resilient is because they are loyal—and not just to me. They're loyal to the company, its mission, and best of all, each other. It's one of the things I love most about the people I work with.

I rolled out the red carpet to get Jim and AJ here, but I've also continued to give them spot bonuses and increase their pay when their performance is particularly stellar. The same is true of other high performers. I like to host a dinner at the end of the year, celebrating the successes of our most valued team members. At the last dinner, we invited about thirty Axon employees and their spouses to a high-end restaurant and gave *everyone* an entire set of smart home devices. The year before that, we gave them top-of-the-line customized wireless headphones.

Then there are the truly exceptional awards for exceptional performances. It's one of my favorite things about working at Axon—we do not shy away from recognizing and rewarding our employees in memorable ways. Other examples include designer handbags, Rolex watches, and when the occasion calls for it, cars.

This is not to say that we buy our employees' loyalty—these things aren't given simply to make them like us. It doesn't work that way. The point is that if you're going to go over the top to get them here, you better make damn sure you continue to make them feel appreciated when they're doing the excellent work you hired them to do.

If you don't? Someone else is going to roll out the red carpet for them.

To be clear, it's not just about material rewards. I spend roughly two-thirds of my time on people—listening to their challenges, coaching them, giving them career advice, or talking to my direct reports at length about their own teams. I do formal in-depth people reviews with my staff about twice a year, but informally and to a lesser degree approximately twice a month. More than offering material things, I like to show my team my appreciation by being generous with my time.

Part of showing your appreciation for them is supporting their growth—even if that means their growth occurs by taking a higher position somewhere else. I reassure my team constantly that if they ever get the call from another company to take a CFO position or something similar that I would support them if they wanted to take it. I would support them without question because it's good for them, their family, and their career. I truly believe that the best of us help others achieve their dreams and aspirations unconditionally.

The recruiters *have* come calling for members of my team. And while I'd readily champion their ascent up the corporate ladder, they've stayed. They genuinely feel our appreciation of them and see that we're invested in their growth, no matter where they end up. I've made sure that my senior leadership is constantly in the orbit of the executive team, getting their voice heard and feeling like they have a seat at the table—because they do, and I love to see them shine when they have that opportunity.

What's even better for me than *seeing* them shine is *hearing* how they shine. I not only make sure my team has a seat at the table; I encourage them to interact directly with the rest of the executive team, our board, and even outside parties such as investors or journalists without me. I ask them to simply keep me informed as to anything I should know but tell them to not get bogged down with bureaucracy waiting for me to approve some communication or key message they need to get across. It's so rewarding for me when I hear these other stakeholders gushing about the rock stars on my team.

You can't feel threatened by the idea that your team might outshine you. If you do, you can't be an effective leader, and you can't build an ironclad team. Let go of your ego. When your team shines, it reflects on your abilities as a leader to bring talented people together. It also creates an environment where your people feel safe. It's a lot harder to leave a space where you're comfortable and secure.

LIKE VELCRO

Their loyalty to me is only one connection. I have singular connections to my direct reports.

But then they have connections with each other and have fostered loyalty among themselves. That then trickles down to their own teams, and they all end up building the same mindset and mentality. It's one of the reasons I encourage people to stay out of their silos. Wear multiple hats. Work between the different functions wherever you're needed and without direction from a micromanager. Know that you've got the trust from your team to spread your wings and get the job done right.

It results not only in loyalty, but a camaraderie that makes the loyalty that much stronger. We notice when someone is having a down day or if they're encountering a rough patch of work, and we link arms to figure out how we can help. When you create those kinds of bonds, you have to work very hard to pull them apart.

Like Velcro.

I'm unendingly proud of the resiliency of my team because it passed the ultimate stress test. We'll talk about exactly how in the conclusion.

CONCLUSION

"IN JAWAD WE TRUST"

Let me take you back to October of 2017, when the shit had hit the fan.

My team is in full-on crisis-management mode. The threats of lawsuits are piling up.

Enter Isaiah, who at the time was transitioning into the interim general counsel role.

Isaiah is very pragmatic. He doesn't get emotional about things. When the rest of us are wringing our hands, he looks at things very objectively. The lawsuit threats kept coming, and I was panicked, and at one point, I asked what our exposure would be if we were to actually get sued. It was said that if we looked at the dip in the stock price and factored in a class action lawsuit from a large number of shareholders, we could be looking at a significant financial exposure.

That figure did nothing to help my anxiety.

Isaiah was as cool as the proverbial cucumber. "We have insurance to cover just this kind of thing. It's not ideal, but it's out of our control. Let's worry about what we can control, which is getting our response back to the SEC."

It was during this time that Isaiah and Jim formed a tight bond. The response to the SEC was not only about our accounting practices, which was the basis of their questions. We also had to make sure that what we disclosed and how we disclosed it didn't open us up to any other liability from a legal standpoint. Isaiah brought in the right outside counsel to help ensure that.

Even Jim was a little shell-shocked, but Isaiah was the calm hand at the wheel, helping us navigate our way through the SEC while attempting to shoot down the threat of potential shareholder lawsuits.

We flubbed the initial explanation of what happened. When we did, it was Isaiah who told us we needed to come right out and be transparent about what occurred with my spam filters, and it was immensely helpful. Being forthcoming with that information was instrumental in avoiding those lawsuits. That, along with Isaiah and Jim working on the SEC response, allowed me to turn my attention to what would really get them to disappear: getting the stock price to go back up. The upcoming investor day would be my opportunity to achieve that goal.

Meanwhile, AJ was talking to investors, and Jim was scrambling to get our financials under control because we still had a chance to have one of our material weaknesses remediated by the of the year, and we wanted to keep his focus on that.

Before I go further, I want to add a little context to the story.

A 10 PERCENT MISS

I interviewed with Axon in December of 2016. As part of that process, I sat in the executive boardroom and got to listen to the budget presentations for the upcoming year. All the departments made their pitches and their asks, and everyone—everyone—was getting the thumbs-up.

I was sitting next to a gentleman named Arvind, who is today our VP of Finance, when we broke for lunch.

"Hey, I've been in meetings at GE where people got thrown

out of the room for asking for too much in a budget, and here, everyone is getting a thumbs-up. Does anyone ask questions or push back? Is there going to be any debate? Or does everyone just get a greenlight for what they want to spend?"

Arvind shook his head. "We could use some more discipline around our costs."

"Well, how are you doing on your operating expenses this year compared to your budget?"

"We're going to be about $16 million over."

"Help me put that in perspective," I told him.

"Well," he said, "we had a $200-million operating budget. So this was almost a ten percent miss."

I was stunned. "How did that happen?"

"To be honest," he said, "you're the first person to ask me that question all year."

COLLABORATION

Arvind is collaboration personified. He is so good at collaborating that he sometimes has trouble delegating, though he's aware of it.

Recall that he was already here when I started. Some people in leadership said that I should rebuild my finance team and that no one was sacred. There was a stigma that the finance function had not been well built, and when I brought in Jim and AJ, the thought was that the existing team wasn't as strong as who I was bringing in.

That perception could not have been more wrong in Arvind's case.

Immediately, I noticed how many people came to me telling me how much they liked working with Arvind—both existing team members and new people who had come in, even those just starting with the company today.

That fact points to his dedication to the job and his desire to help his team. It's one of the side effects of having all four uncoachable traits— being the type of person who will run through walls to see the business succeed. Arvind always searches for the win-win. He constantly looks to find ways where everyone gets everything they want without having to break rules or break budgets.

Remember, I didn't come up through Wall Street and don't have a CPA. I did bring a solid background in financial planning and analysis (FP&A) to Axon. And a core strength of mine is building models for short- and long-term forecasts, mergers and acquisitions, budgeting—you name it.

I made my name as a CFO driving teams to achieve the financial outcomes in those models. I'd planned to bring a heavy dose of that to Axon.

Except when I got here, I saw what a command Arvind had of our financials and how much trust he engendered. As such, I decided to step back and not tell him how I would have run the FP&A shop but rather empowered him in ways he'd never been empowered before. He's responded by growing into a true business partner who has taken ownership of the P&L. It's personally rewarding to support him the same way I was supported earlier in my career.

Whenever he's involved in problem-solving and decision-making, we end up in a better spot as a company—every time.

Axon was spending their way into oblivion. The top line was growing, but their bottom line was heading south, and it was reflecting in the stock price. This was a material weakness we could fix.

After I took the position as CFO, I worked with Arvind to come up with a budget by department. Arvind was key to helping me come up with an operating budget that everyone could sift through.

If a department wanted forty new employees next year? They didn't get them all on January 1. Was forty even the right number? Maybe they only needed thirty, and maybe that thirty got spread throughout the year. Maybe we wouldn't invest in that flying police car prototype next year. Arvind was instrumental in getting these kinds of disciplines in place in the wake of the October disaster.

Come November, we had an investor day in New York. It had been planned for quite some time, long before the release of the letters from the SEC. It was originally going to be my coming-out party, where I would assert my vision as CFO and put my stamp on the business, talking about what I saw as the financial strategy of the business for the next few years. That plan didn't change, but it took on a new level of importance.

We rented a fancy ballroom in a trendy midtown hotel for the all-day event. Rick talked, Luke talked, along with all of the other executives, saving me for the end of the day. I remember telling AJ that I wanted to go first and get it over with.

"No," she said. "We put you first and people are going to leave after you're done because, make no mistake about it, everyone is here for you. They want to hear your plans for the new financial strategy of the business."

Talk about pressure. Still, she was right. People were there to see if I was the train wreck the press had made me out to be after the SEC incident or if I was going to step up and help bring this company into the future.

I put my game face on and stepped in front of the crowd.

WHY ARE THEY ON THEIR PHONES?

I started with a short overview of myself: who I was, my background, and why I was a fit for the role.

Then I hit them with the details, explaining the new pillars of our financial model.

"We're going to shift the business to recurring cash flows, bundle our products in subscriptions, and invest to expand our total addressable market all while we drive profitability."

I then walked through a presentation that laid out exactly how we were going to accomplish these things. I talked about how software was only a relatively small portion of our business today, but long-term, it was going to account for more than half, and how the other half would be hardware, both on a subscription basis. We talked about TASER weapon service plans and expanding our market; about how we would sell enhanced services, such as cameras in cars, to the 600,000 US law enforcement officers, which would open up an additional 400,000 vehicles.

From there, I went into our plans for global expansion, which would impact pricing and profitability. I explained how our multiyear contracts would be designed to spur renewals and how our margins would go up because of the decreased cost in software in the years when there was no hardware to supply. I discussed the upsell opportunities we'd have over time because we were developing new features to sell.

What really got their attention, though, was when I pointed out that when I arrived at Axon, long-term goals were set, but no one actually measured if we were heading toward those targets, so I wiped the slate clean. It was time to decide where we wanted to be three years from now and work backward to build a plan each year to achieve that.

"By the way," I said, "this isn't just lip service. We changed the company's compensation plan to align with this new direction. Previously, everyone's bonus was tied only to revenue and other sales metrics, so the top line grew, and everyone was getting paid while profitability went down. No one felt the pain. No more."

I noticed some positive murmuring from the audience. I also noticed people on their phones.

"As of today, our TASER weapon business is profitable. For everything else, the word 'investment' is code for 'losing money.' Everything else we're doing is losing us money.

We're going to start shifting that, and we're going to get to overall profitability one product line at a time." I then showed them a timeline of when our body camera, in-car camera, and software product lines would shift from the investment phase to gaining leverage to breaking even to being profitable.

There was a reason everyone was on their phones. The market was still open.

They were buying our stock—it was increasing in value in real time.

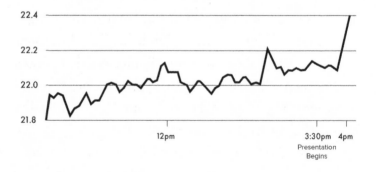

AXON ENTERPRISE INC (NASDAQ: AXON)
INTRADAY CHART FOR NOVEMBER 16, 2017

Whenever there is a public event like an investor day, the stock analysts put out a research note, and they update all the shareholders that bought stock. The research note that J.P. Morgan put out was glowing. It said, "We were impressed with the new CFO, who seems to have already made his mark on AAXN, with a cultural shift underway toward focus on *profitable* growth.

"In Jawad we trust."

IMPOSSIBLE WITHOUT THE TEAM

Having a resilient team made all of this possible.

Arvind came up with the budget. AJ worked to calm investor panic. Jim made sure I could report on our forecasted financials with confidence while working to clean up the material weaknesses. Isaiah helped quell the noise that persisted around potential shareholder lawsuits, which were quickly becoming a remote possibility as our stock price kept rising.

Those whom I reported to, specifically Rick, had my back. I had to look around the table at our executive team and say, "What I'm going to do is completely different from what you're used to. I'm going to change the way things are done here, and it's going to mean I'm going to say no to you sometimes, and you have to be okay with that."

Every one of them said, "Let's do it."

I had been a part of this organization, a member of this team, for a little more than six months. Chances are that anyone else would have washed their hands of me when the SEC crisis struck. Their company's name was being dragged through the mud, and they had to make a decision about whether they trusted me or not. It was a precarious position to be in, and yet I heard none of that doubt. None of that mistrust.

Everyone rallied and said, "Let's focus, get this presentation dialed in, and turn this thing around."

The lessons I learned on my leadership journey helped me to surround myself with a resilient team I could trust and who trusted me.

PRINCIPLES IN ACTION

If the team had seen me panicking, they would have panicked. Yes, it was a shock to the system the day it all went down, but "composure" was the word of the day. I knew we could get through it if calm was maintained. In fact, I poked fun at myself in front of them, which opened the door for them to do it too. To this day, Jim still makes fun of my email spam filter, telling people to be sure not to send follow-ups to my email.

I knew that after the initial shock, it was crucial for me to remove myself from the situation and look at things objectively. We had to put together a crisis communications team, and I had to stop worrying about saving face—because I did at first. It was personally hurtful for me to see the headlines in the news that seemed to single me out, and to bear the brunt of this when there were others who held blame in this as well. I wasn't going to fire the receptionist who didn't put through the call or the finance employee who forgot to register my name with the SEC.

This was the time to set that all aside and acknowledge that this was bigger than my reputation. I had to do what was best for the company and act out of integrity. I believe that, ultimately, the investors appreciated that I didn't attempt to explain things away and instead owned it. The email was sent to me. I had to reflect the uncoachable qualities of integrity and accountability not only to them but to my team.

I also took into account that perception was reality at this stage. It didn't matter what I knew the truth to be in this situation. What they saw is what they believed. The investors' first data point on me is that I was selected as CFO of Axon, and the next thing they know, I'm in trouble with the SEC. I'm sure there were still some people within our company who shared that view, and I can't blame them. It's why I opened my presentation on investor day with a slide about who I was. I needed to shift their perception to get them to embrace what I had planned for the future.

In doing so, I made sure not to drape myself in roses. I was up-front and self-critical. As part of that accountability, I showed them with confidence how I was going to fix what had gone wrong—that we could grow our revenue *and* improve our profitability. The two did not need to be mutually exclusive.

Part of that entailed playing the heavy with our executive team. I told them that we were going to stand up in front of the world and tell everyone that this was our new financial strategy, and I reminded them that meant hearing no from me more often than they were used to. This wouldn't work if they didn't commit, and they did.

Had I not relentlessly and aggressively pursued talent, I would not have been able to surround myself with a loyal, tough, and persistent team—one that would not abandon me in the trenches. Because I was able to lean so heavily on them, they in turn felt valued, not just by me but the organization as a whole. It is through their efforts that we made it through that trying time and why our team is now stronger than ever before.

THE MOST IMPORTANT THING THEY DIDN'T TELL ME

At this stage in my journey, perhaps something has become evident to you.

If the early part of my career was defined by *how* I reacted and responded to what happened to me, the later part was defined by *whom* I surrounded myself with. The people I worked for, worked with, and hired on my teams have been the single most important factors *by far* in terms of my career turning out the way it has.

The further you advance in your career, the more important it is that you learn how to lead and drive change through influencing. Building relationships and coalitions are among the most important thing that you can do.

A mentor told me once, when I was transitioning from an individual contributor to a manager, that there was a limit to how much I can get done with just my laptop and myself, and that I would need to learn how to build great teams if I wanted to continue to find success. It was advice that seemed obvious at the time but is something I've thought back to often the more I've learned it to be true.

However good you are at any given task, however skilled you are, or however smart you are is irrelevant in the grand scheme if you are unable to build and maintain high-performing teams, and there is no higher-performing team than the one that is able to continue to perform at that high level in the face of adversity.

An effective team that is not resilient will only carry you so far. When faced with adversity, they won't be there for you in the way you need them when you need them the most.

The four uncoachable traits that I've referred to in this book—integrity, accountability, collaboration, and positivity—are individually important factors for building resilient teams. Collectively, however, they serve as a heuristic for something that is probably the most important factor in building resilient teams and is itself an uncoachable trait: trust.

If you've identified someone with the types of traits that will allow you to trust them, then trust them. Don't micromanage them. If they have the skills, and they embody the traits that you know you can't coach, let them spread their wings and give them room to fly. Chances are, they'll fly more often than crash, but—and this is equally important—it's *okay* if they crash. It's okay to let your team fail. As you've seen by now, I failed continually during the course of my career, over and over and over again, and I learned far more from those failures than I did from my successes.

If you're telling your team what to do and how to do it, they'll never learn for themselves. Give them a broad objective and let them figure out their own path to success.

Make no mistake, I'm not saying to manage in absentia.

Be there for your team to guide them, coach them, and provide them with air cover when they need it. But know this: the bargain of trust requires two willing participants, and your team won't trust you if you won't trust them.

If you want to build an effective team, hire for skills. If you want to build a resilient team, hire people you can trust. If you want to leave a mark on this world, hire for both.

BELIEVE IN YOURSELF, OR NO ONE ELSE WILL

If I could go back and tell the version of myself at the beginning of all of this—the one who heard he didn't belong in this company or that position—I'd tell him to just believe in himself.

And that's what I want to tell you.

You might have perceptions of the leaders you read about and think that never in a million years could you ever be like them, that you could be an executive in a publicly traded company or a solid midlevel manager or whatever your leadership goal might be.

That was my perception. Never in a million years.

I assumed that those types of roles were reserved for people that come from a different walk of life. People that had different opportunities afforded to them. That didn't look like me. That didn't share my faith.

I'm here to tell you it's bullshit. You *can* do it.

Yes, the path is paved for some. It's an unfortunate reality, but it's true. However, there is nothing to say that you can't create your own path.

But you don't have to do it alone.

If you aspire to leadership and you want to build the types of teams around you like the one I have, then I want to hear from you. At Axon, I am the diversity and inclusiveness sponsor, and I view championing that agenda as one of the most important aspects of my role as a leader. Our underrepresented communities are looking to forge their way into corporate America. They no longer simply want to be tapped on the shoulder and told which direction to go. They want to find their own North Star.

This was my story and my experiences, but my way to this destination was not the only one. Visit me at JawadAhsan. com and tell me about your goals and aspirations.

I want to hear your story.

Let me be a member of your resilient team.

ACKNOWLEDGMENTS

In a way, this book is partially an acknowledgment of my failures and the people I've failed throughout my career so far. Some of those people were caring, some were not, but everyone gave me feedback that was invaluable—intentional or not. I thank you for that feedback and for fueling a fire for impact through leadership that grows hotter every day.

This book is also a deep expression of gratitude to those who have supported me. I know that I tend to focus the vast majority of my energy and thoughts on my detractors and have been maniacally motivated to prove them wrong. The truth is, however, that my supporters far outweigh my detractors, and I am exceedingly fortunate to have the network of support that I do.

I never realized until I had kids of my own how hard it is to take time out to attend various sports practices, games, school activities, playdates, camps—the list goes on. And attending is one thing, but being present and engaging in every detail your little one wants to revisit and discuss is real work. I only now fully appreciate just how amazing my parents were as I was growing up—they are present in all of my fondest memories, and their constant coaching and counseling set me up for a lifetime of giving and getting feedback. Mom and Abbu, I love you more than you could possibly know, and hope that I have made you proud.

Being a parent is one of the hardest things I've ever done. I've worked very hard to develop skills for giving feedback and coaching and motivating people through the toughest of challenges, and they are all completely useless every time my two boys both want a blue popsicle and there is only one left. Parenting is such a unique leadership challenge and is so much higher stakes than anything most of us do at work. I'm so fortunate to be married to Arsala, an incredible mother and wife, whose support has made so much of my career and my accomplishments possible. You've supported and encouraged me on every endeavor I've undertaken over the past decade, and this book would not have been possible without you. I love you and am so grateful to be on this journey with you.

When I first had the idea to write a book, I would frequent

libraries and bookstores (more than I already do—libraries and bookstores are my sanctuary) and scan the business section for books by authors like me—sitting C-suite executives who were sharing their stories and lessons learned. Aside from the exceedingly rare Sheryl Sandberg–esque rock-star executive, there aren't many of these books out there. There are lots of books by writers, bloggers, speakers, former executives, or some combination thereof. The reason for this is simple: the demands placed on the time of a public-company executive are enormous. While I sacrificed what little personal time I did have—as well as sleep—to write this book, the truth is I wouldn't have been able to do it without my team at Scribe Media.

John Vercher, we formed an instant connection and were not only able to move at the speed of trust but of cultural understanding as well. I could not have been more perfectly paired with you and am looking forward to continuing our partnership. Kacy Wren, you were the steady hand at the wheel of this project. So many times, when I doubted myself, and the direction we were headed, I found myself reaching for my phone to call you first. Cindy Curtis, Rachael Brandenburg, Rikki Jump—thank you all for your patience and diligence as we navigated through this project.

Throughout this book were examples of my learnings in action via my team at Axon. There is no shortage of adjectives I could use to describe my time at Axon so far—magical, transformative, amazing, fun, breathtaking, eye-opening, insightful, rewarding, fulfilling—and I would apply every one of those adjectives to my experience with my team as well.

Andrea James and Angel Ambrosio, you are, pound for pound, the most dynamic tandem I have ever witnessed in my professional career. What the two of you have accomplished so far together, and the value you have generated, is nothing short of incredible. Thank you both for the constant feedback and input you provided along the way.

Jim Zito, you're a bastion of integrity and a master of your domain. Axon is a better company because of you. Arvind Bobra, your relentless work ethic and collaborative problem-solving have kept us on the path we laid out for ourselves. As we navigate our way to twelve tranches, you are charting the way. Isaiah Fields, we often discuss how the frequency and severity of legal issues we've faced as a company is unprecedented in corporate America, and what may not be apparent to you is that you're a big part of the reason we are able to successfully navigate those issues. I'm always grateful for your counsel, despite it being tough to hear sometimes.

To my newer team members, whom I've only started working with but have quickly earned my trust—Mark

Wachtmann, Mike Rennie, Henrik Kuhl, David Waxberg, Matt Angorn, and Bonnie Emmet—I'm excited for the journey ahead that we've embarked on together.

To my entire organization, I put everything I've learned in my life and career into handpicking you to be a part of my team. I owe you a debt of gratitude for putting your trust in me and hope you understand after reading this book why I wake up every day to work toward repaying that debt.

To Rick and to Axon's incredible board of directors, thank you for the unwavering support and guidance. I came to Axon to help you make the bullet obsolete and bring advanced technologies to law enforcement and see now that this is only the first step toward changing the world. I'm inspired by you on a daily basis and humbled to be a part of this team and this mission.

To Luke and Josh, we took this plunge together, and I can't imagine anyone else I would have taken it with. Here's to many more plunges together.

Jeff and Leslie, you're recent additions to the Axon team but have already had an impact, and I know you will be integral to how our story unfolds from here.

I find enormous fulfillment in giving of myself to others who are in pursuit of personal and professional development—my time, advice, energy, and so on. I've done this for so long and to such a degree that I haven't had enough time to invest into maintaining my friendships, which is one of the melancholies of my life.

Having said that, there are friends near and dear to me that I consulted throughout the writing of this book and were invaluable in their advice and guidance. Sofija Jovic, Diana Ganz, Inga Lennes, Kishan Shah, Gabe Stacy, Matt Marsh, and Howie McKibbon, I'm grateful for your input and even more grateful for your friendship.

I am grateful to the institutions that shaped me and my views on leadership. From Billerica Memorial High School, I learned the meaning of grit, and it was here that my competitive fires were first lit. From the College of the Holy Cross, I learned the importance of selflessness, of being men and women for others, and it was here that the seeds of integrity and accountability were first planted in me. From GE, I learned the importance of personal energy and execution, and how to lead and drive change on a large scale through influencing. From MIT, I learned that innovation is nothing if not first principled, that perseverance is more important than raw intelligence, and that, perhaps most importantly, how to frame the question is the most important part of answering the question.

Finally, to my two boys, Ezz and Dia, I am so grateful for

the joy you have brought into our lives and for being the inspiration for this book in the first place. I've watched in amazement as your personalities and your own leadership traits have emerged at the tender ages of six and two and have realized that I have a responsibility to pass on what I've learned. I have so much more to share and couldn't be prouder of you or more excited to share it.

ABOUT THE AUTHOR

At age twenty-nine, **JAWAD AHSAN** defined his North Star: he wanted to move up to the C-suite. A year later, he became a divisional CFO at GE Healthcare and was soon promoted to be a GE executive. By age thirty-four, he was the CFO of a private-equity-backed SaaS company, and by age thirty-seven, became the CFO of a publicly traded company, Axon. As CFO, Jawad is responsible for leading the company's Global Finance, Corporate Strategy, Legal, and IT organizations, as well as Axon's consumer-facing business. During his tenure, Axon's market cap has increased from $1 billion to over $6 billion.

Made in the USA
Monee, IL
22 March 2021